THE DEADLY SNAKES

REAL ROCK AND ROLL TONIGHT

The Rise and Gentle Fall of Canada's Greatest Band

THE DEADLY SNAKES

REAL ROCK AND ROLL TONIGHT

J.B. STANIFORTH

Invisible Publishing
Halifax & Toronto

Library and Archives Canada Cataloguing in Publication

Staniforth, J. B. (Jesse B.)
      The Deadly Snakes : real rock and roll tonight / J.B. Staniforth.

(Bibliophonic ; 3)
ISBN 978-1-926743-29-5

      1. Deadly Snakes (Musical group). 2. Rock musicians--Canada--Biography. I. Title. II. Series: Bibliophonic ; 3

ML421.D278S78 2012   782.42166092'2   C2012-907423-3

Cover illustration/Design by

Designed by Megan Fildes | Typeset in Laurentian and Slate
With thanks to type designer Rod McDonald

Printed and bound in Canada

Invisible Publishing | Halifax & Toronto
www.invisiblepublishing.com

We acknowledge the support of the Canada Council for the Arts which last year invested $20.1 million in writing and publishing throughout Canada.

Invisible Publishing recognizes the support of the Province of Nova Scotia through the Department of Communities, Culture & Heritage. We are pleased to work in partnership with the Culture Division to develop and promote our cultural resources for all Nova Scotians.

This is for Chris Jones, with boundless gratitude.

It's also in memory of my dear, departed Djuna Cat,
who always sat beside me as I wrote.

INTRODUCTION

FOR MUCH OF North America, garage rock as a genre happened in 2001, somewhere between the release of the White Stripes' *White Blood Cells* LP in July and the appearance of the Hives' breakthrough "Main Offender" single from *Veni Vidi Vicious* in September. However, by that point, garage rock was very nearly finished for many of the people who'd been following the genre for a decade or more. For several years, garage stacks in record stores had been positively glutted with uninspired releases by underwhelming bands. For many who had been garage rock purists, as the turn of the millennium approached, the only bands and releases that merited notice were those that were truly stunning—like the White Stripes record, or the first Deadly Snakes LP. These two debut LPs, incidentally, were released within a month of one another on the same label in 1999.

As a delineated genre, garage rock had been around for nearly 40 years in various incarnations, though the punk rock thrust of the sound that would eventually lead to releases by the Snakes, the White Stripes and the Hives (among others) began in the late 80s with bands like the Gories, the Mono Men, the Devil Dogs and Billy Childish's various groups (including Thee Headcoats and Thee Mighty Caesars).

I had the good fortune of growing up in Ottawa, which by the mid-90s was home to a prolific garage punk scene, particularly thanks to the cultivation efforts of John Westhaver, who ran the city's best record store (Birdman Sound), fronted local garage punk quartet Resin Scraper and booked showcases of local garage bands at Bumper's Roadhouse and the Dominion Tavern. By 1996, there were numerous bands playing garage-inflected punk and rock and roll in Ottawa— including the Stand GT, the Black Boot Trio, the Knurlings, the Speedy Huffler Kings[1] and the Dead City Rebels.[2]

John Westhaver's store introduced me to the Gories, the Oblivians, Thee Headcoats, the Dwarves, the Supersuckers and the New Bomb Turks, along with many other excellent bands like the Devil Dogs and Spain's berserk Los Ass-Draggers. I was in my late teens in the 90s and had spent a few years in the punk scene, which was by that point contorted in political cramps. Ottawa was especially political, with its thriving scene of "emo" bands (who'd be unrecognizable to fans of

---

1 Whose very promising existence was cut short by the overdose death of their singer/bassist Uri Guthrie, an inveterate solid dude, in early 1997. Older than me by a couple of years at an age when those things mattered much more, Uri always seemed like "an older punk"; he was 22 when he died.

2 I had the pleasure of forming the Dead City Rebels (then called the Catholic School Boys) in 1995 with singer Neill "Butchie" Peterson and bassist René "Son of Lionel" LeClair, two refugees from rural New Brunswick, and J-P Sadek, the son of an Egyptian bookseller, before my eventual and necessary replacement by two guys who could each play guitar far better than I could. The unreleased LP they recorded for Man's Ruin records is one of the great lost Canadian rock and roll albums. As Simon Harvey who runs the collector punk label Ugly Pop said recently, "It's a garage record from Ottawa in the 90s. No collectors are going to be interested in that right now, but wait 10 or 15 years and people will be falling over one another for the chance to put it out."

that genre today)—serious young men in mechanic's jackets who made their own soy milk and occasionally cried on stage while playing loud, angular, cryptic music about, for example, the oppression of East Timor. It's not that I didn't agree with their politics—I did—but the stultifying self-consciousness of it all was a little much for a 17-year-old who wanted huge, loud music that reflected enormous, confused emotions.

That was how I fell into garage rock, which was defiantly apolitical, and whose prime message was one of swaggering self-confidence. More than anything else happening at the time, it *sounded cool*. I couldn't listen to songs like "Young-blood" by Thee Headcoats, "No Butter for My Bread" by the Oblivians, "Poor" by the Supersuckers or "Id Slips In" by the New Bomb Turks without channelling their sneering attitude—and playing those records *loud*.

I missed the Turks on their first tour through Ottawa in '94—during which they played at the now-legendary minis-cule emo stronghold 5 Arlington—but two years later they played at Oliver's Pub at Carleton University. Their show was a revelation. By that point I'd gotten used to high-quality garage punk on a regular basis, but watching manic front-man Eric Davidson make fun of mohawked punkers in the crowd while himself tearing up the stage, I was convinced that garage rock was the most relevant thing happening in music. It felt like pure rebellion—rebelling even against the predictability of punk—drawing on the blues-based rock and roll of greasers and juvenile delinquents, speeding it up and making it even more snarling and snotty.

Garage rock wasn't that far off from other permutations of punk rock, and—outside bands that reproduced the high reverb, low fidelity, bluesy sounds of 60s garage—even a purist would be hard pressed to say precisely what separates the best tracks from the Rip Offs or the Turks from straight-up punk rock or early hardcore. But garage punk in the 90s filled a vacuum that had appeared as a result of a variety of factors in the punk scene. One of these was the emergence of emo and math rock, which brought along with it an excruciating obsession with appropriate politics; another was the degeneration of hardcore into beefy mosh-metal by puritan dudes barking about how they didn't drink milk. Between the huge successes of Green Day and the Offspring in the summer of 1994, fanciers of pop punk suddenly had to contend with a wave of copycat bands who diluted the genre until it no longer seemed to reflect any originality. Dopey street punk already seemed silly, and crust punk, with a few exceptions (notably Chicago's mighty Los Crudos), seemed trite and uniform. If you were young, pissed off, confused, and wanted loud, fast music that made you feel bad ass, then garage rock was something that rang true: it sounded fresh, fun and obnoxious, and it spoke to me.

I was not alone. In the U.S., the labels Crypt Records, Sympathy for the Record Industry, Rip Off, Estrus, Norton and Get Hip! were moving considerable units and consequently able to sign a spate of new bands every year. When I moved to Montreal to go to university in the fall of '96, I fell into that city's garage scene, which was anchored to the Jailhouse Rock Café, seeing the Infernos (featuring Paul Spence, who'd eventually play in the Daylight Lovers and the CPC Gangbangs, and write/star in the films *FUBAR* and *FUBAR 2*), Tricky Woo and the Scat Rag Boosters. I wore a leather jacket and bought virtually every record I could afford that came out on Crypt or Estrus or Sympathy.

That was fine for a couple of years—and then, abruptly, it got boring. In maybe '98, Spokane, Washington's the Makers played at Jailhouse Rock, looking like preening clowns in their dopey haircuts and 60s uniforms. Their set was appalling. It had none of the fun or energy of the bands I really liked—instead, it reminded me of the anaemic flaccidity of hair metal that drove me to punk rock.

Then there was the summer of 1999, during which I made the terrible mistake of buying a stack of records based only on their receiving positive reviews in *Hit List* magazine. Around that time, I decided I never wanted to hear any dude in a bowling shirt singing about cars or 50s movie monsters or bad women or hard-livin' again. I didn't want to see a band of four guys with dyed-black hair and full sleeves of tattoos playing a cover of the MC5, the Stooges or the Sonics. I definitely didn't want to hear a band covering some 60s frat rock group's cover of a blues song. Garage rock became to me, almost overnight, brutally and miserably predictable.

I hadn't been alone in seeking solace in garage punk, I wasn't alone in turning my back on it either. Most notably, the New Bomb Turks pilloried the entire genre and its tired conventions in the feral track "Point A to Point Blank," which opened their 2000 release *Nightmare Scenario*.[3] In that track, they mocked the garage scene as a collection of nerds "play-

---

3 *Nightmare Scenario* was a strikingly bleak and nihilistic record the Turks produced following the death of frontman Eric Davidson's father; its entire range of lyrics dealt with despair and alienation, including alienation from the scene that supported the band.

ing dress-up white trash" who "switched Spock for Pebbles comps," and concluded "Bettie Page and Satan tattoos only hold up for so long." That hit home for me, naming precisely the shallow artifice that disgusted me about the garage scene.

Of course, those garage records I loved—the Turks, the Gories, the Oblivians and other highlights—still sounded great. It wasn't even that the form itself had become so excruciating, but the lack of imagination in the paint-by-numbers bands carrying its mantle had killed garage punk dead.

This wasn't good news. I had no idea what records to buy now; I returned to hardcore and pop-edged punk rock, while finally beginning to explore the emo and math rock I'd ignored a few years before. It became significantly harder to enjoy straight-up rock and roll, which I think was the case for a lot of people in those years. I began to avoid shows featuring bands described as "garage" or "sleaze," for which, a few years before, I would have instantly marked my calendar.

For that reason, I didn't pay any attention when *Love Undone*, the first Deadly Snakes LP, came out. I associated the band with Montreal's the Spaceshits, and I had only seen those guys once. They opened for the New Bomb Turks in April '97 at Montreal's infamous Foufounes Électriques (where the sound was so bad that though I knew the entire Turks' catalogue back to front, I still couldn't identify half the songs they played) and managed to play their entire set without being able to finish a single number. I recall—maybe incorrectly—that Spaceshits members threw beer bottles at the crowd from the stage, and that seemed to me to be tiresome, predictable theatrics. Afterward, their guitarist hit on my girlfriend while I was holding her hand. I can't say I was thrilled about that either.

Prejudiced against the Spaceshits, and a pioneer of internet shit-talk, I took to decrying them on usenet—without having heard their impressive debut LP on Sympathy, which was every bit as good as people said it was. At the time, their frontman Mark Sultan (aka BBQ) was pretty pissed off at me, and he had reason to be—they were a killer band that I wrote off after one show without even hearing their record. I kept running my mouth until '99, when I struck up a conversation with a friendly dude on a bus in a Rip Offs T-shirt who later revealed he was in the Spaceshits (Danny Marks, a killer drummer who later went on to play with the Sexareenos and the CPC Gangbangs); I then felt appropriately awful. Danny always seemed like a nice guy, and I don't think he's ever played in a bad band.

Nonetheless, I was still knee-deep in my grudge against the Spaceshits when the Snakes started up, and I didn't see them live until Labour Day weekend of 2001, when they played the Jailhouse backed by Greg "Oblivian" Cartwright. By that point, I'd had their debut LP recommended to me by several extremely reliable sources, notably ex-*Maximumrocknroll* columnist and "shitworker" Lali Donovan, who insistently championed them as one of the strongest bands playing the genre. Lali is rarely wrong about bands, so I intended to see them straight away. When they turned up a block from my house, I rushed over and was taken aback by the Snakes' bristling energy versus Cartwright's more sedate (or heavily sedated) stage presence. They were exciting, chaotic, and young and that was precisely what I wanted in a rock and roll band.

By that point in 2001, I'd been through a number of significant emotional upheavals, and had decided that what I needed more than anything was the driving force of unpretentious rock and roll to provide me the impetus I needed to keep going. The Snakes made it immediately clear that they could supply the energy I required, and underlined it all the more in the liner notes of *Love Undone*, where they threw down the gauntlet for appearance rock bands like the Makers and the Black Halos in a short essay that stated that the album was, "a rally call to abandon irony and play from your soul—to be young and to be bold." That was precisely what I was still looking for: badass rock and roll without shtick or irony, confident that the power of the music would say everything it needs to.

Another thing I loved about the record was the liner notes, which proudly read, "The Deadly Snakes – Toronto." Never had there been a band that represented Toronto so much, in all its conflicting glory; never had I known a band that had grown up in Toronto and had allowed the city to permeate their songs. An ex-Ottawan in Montreal, I nonetheless understood the importance of regionalism and representing one's home town, however messy and absurd it might be. I liked *Love Undone* immensely and immediately, and my feelings about the record never changed.

A couple of years later, I visited my dear friend Bobby Lotz in the middle of the night at CKUT-FM, where he hosted a show egregiously (sorry, Bob) called "Sexy Like Make-Believe."

"Have you heard the new Deadly Snakes album?" he asked breathlessly, referring to 2003's *Ode to Joy*. I'd tried the record a few times myself at the radio station but couldn't wrap my head around its minimalist approach—loud, hard songs sometimes broken down to only two or three instruments, equally troubled by the sudden emergence of organist Max McCabe-Lokos as a singer. For all its simplicity, *Ode to Joy* wasn't an album I could access immediately. I told Bobby as much, but he shook his head.

"You've *got to* give it another try," he said. "This is something special."

He played a track for me—I think it was "Oh My Bride"—and I had to agree that, despite the song's instrumentation consisting only of one loud guitar, a bass drum, tambourines and handclaps, it was absolutely killer. This deconstruction was a reaction to precisely the same kind of tedium that I had myself felt about garage rock. None of those songs sounded like the product of a band with sleeve-tattoos and Beatle-boots. Rather, this sounded like some young guys from Toronto singing about what was on their minds, using the tools they'd developed over the previous two records. *Ode to Joy* was noisy, messy and layered, and however difficult it was to approach at first, it held up to repeated listening like virtually no garage punk record I'd heard before—probably because it was no longer a garage record, but rather a Deadly Snakes album.

By the time the *Porcella* LP was released in 2005, I knew to be on the lookout for something important, but was nonetheless surprised by the album's grim understatement and fixation on death and aging, issues that sat uncomfortably close to home for me as I was approaching 30 with no clear sense of what I should be doing with myself.

In the fall of 2005, I admitted to myself that I hated my chosen career of teaching college and finally began to see a psychologist to talk about the turmoil of feelings about the job that I had spent five years working toward only to realize I couldn't do. My shrink appointments were on Friday nights at eight or nine, and somehow early on I got into the habit of listening to *Porcella* as I came away from them. That album was precisely the soundtrack that I needed—an uneasy, eerie and emotional document that didn't quite make sense to me. The songs that Max McCabe-Lokos (under the moniker "Age of Danger") sang in his by turns vulnerable and stagy tenor—notably the incredible "Gore Veil" and the pair of quasi-existential album closers "The Banquet" and "A Bird in the Hand is Worthless"—spoke especially to me, but so did André Ethier's stirring and powerful "Oh Lord, My Heart." None of these songs sounded healthy or stable, but they sounded alive, and that combination of feelings was a clear reflection of how I inevitably felt as I came out of my shrink's office and crossed the ice-crusted snow of Parc Lafontaine, processing the various discussions of the preceding hour.

As Bobby had said to me before of *Ode to Joy*, I inevitably described *Porcella* as "something special" when I was trying to convince my friends to buy it. Later, when Max and André listed the album's influences (Nico, Leonard Cohen, Van Morrison—all of them far removed from the influences of moribund garage punk), it would make sense to me that the album hadn't come from nowhere. But at the time, it sounded entirely new, vulnerable, true and on the edge of crazy—and it sounded fantastic. I needed that album and I clung to it, because it felt to me like a reflection of honesty I could rely upon at a time when I couldn't rely on shit when it came to myself or my future.

At the same time, I couldn't imagine how the band could

follow *Porcella*, and I was not at all surprised the next year to hear that they had no plans to do anything of the sort—they were to break up at the end of the summer. Bobby emailed me from Toronto, where he'd moved, frantic that I needed to come down for the last Snakes' shows, and I helplessly replied that I was, as always, completely broke and entirely desperate. I could barely pay for groceries and rent, let alone afford to leave town to see a band I loved break up. Accordingly, I missed the last two Deadly Snakes shows, which Bobby described as the best he had ever seen. While I was terribly disappointed, I wasn't surprised about that either— years of being broke prepare you for those sorts of let-downs.

And anyway, I had the records, which sincerely seemed to grow in depth and meaning with each passing year. I was a proselytizer for the Snakes, selling rock and roll fans on their first two LPs while suggesting the last two records to folks who might like something a little poppier, a little darker, a little more introspective. I wanted everyone I knew to hear those albums in part because I wanted the band to receive the recognition they'd never gotten when they were together.

I don't know whether my constant recommendations had any success in keeping the reputation of the Deadly Snakes alive, but to a great extent the need to support them is precisely what drove me to write this book—the desire to see Canada's greatest rock and roll band finally get the praise that was due to them. Who cares if they didn't work for it, didn't suck up to the music press or hire a publicist and appear in fashion ads? While they existed, they were the best band in the country. They sang for themselves, about themselves and their lives. True to their promise, they abandoned irony and played from the soul, and the sound of the Deadly Snakes was the sound of being precisely young, and precisely bold.

They were a fantastic band, and it was an honour when I learned they were willing to help me write this book about them. By all means read it, but if you haven't heard the records, do yourself a favour and get them immediately. Until you've heard them, you've missed some of the best music to ever come out of this country—and, to borrow a line from André Ethier, that's a burn on you.

CHAPTER 1
THE BANQUET

"It was one of the best times of my life. I *loved* it."
– Max McCabe-Lokos

IN THE LATE summer of 2005, Toronto's celebrated garage soul combo the Deadly Snakes gathered for 10 days in a rural Ontario cabin to record their album *Porcella*. Though nobody said so at the time, each of the band's six members knew that it would be the last time they made a record together. It was still more than a year before they'd play their final shows, but even in the cabin each young man knew already what he would eventually admit to his bandmates: touring and sharing a stage wasn't fun anymore, and they feared losing the friendships that had been the band's core since its inception a decade before.

There are hints of the Snakes' coming end throughout *Porcella*, a rich and moody album larded with sadness and resignation. Yet each member of the group recalls the time spent in the cabin recording the record as a blissful interlude. Singer/organist Max McCabe-Lokos says of the *Porcella* session, "It was one of the best times of my life. I *loved* it." The atmosphere of satiation and constant practice in the cabin, he maintains, worked magic on his musical ability. "The things my hands were doing, that I didn't even know I could do, by the end of it, were amazing. I was doing stuff that I didn't even understand how I was playing." Piecing together an album whose lyrical themes dealt with emptiness, regret, and the dread of growing old, the band drank fine wines and spirits and dined every night on huge and sumptuous meals.

It's the prosciutto, though, that first comes to mind when any ex-Snake talks about the recording of *Porcella*: McCabe-Lokos acquired an entire leg of cured pork as the session's icon of excess. He hung it directly over the mixing board and left a knife nearby, allowing anyone passing to cut a piece for himself as he wished. Engineer Josh Bauman recalls he began each morning by wiping up the puddle of pork grease that had dripped onto the cover of the mixing board overnight.

The week's rhythm drifted easily between playing, recording and feasting. Because many of his parts wouldn't be recorded until later on, saxophonist Jeremi Madsen used his downtime to make food runs into town and prepare enormous meals as the rest of the band put songs to tape.

"At the end of laying down a bunch of bed tracks, we'd walk into the kitchen and Jer'd have these incredible meals ready for us," says drummer Andrew Moszynski. The band went so far as to list dinner highlights in the album's liner notes, including baked trout stuffed with sorrel, wild mushrooms à la bordelaise, black pudding, crêpes with sabayon sauce and beer can chicken.

That they should outgrow their juvenile disarray and develop adult tastes is not remarkable in itself. What is surprising about the career of the Deadly Snakes is that not only did they use the turmoil of growing up as the foundation for four critically acclaimed records, but they continued improving as they drew to the end of their arc, and incredibly broke down the band without ending the boyhood friendships that had struggled through a decade in pursuit of rock and roll. Despite the sustained conflict between passive lead singer/guitarist André Ethier and hot-blooded singer/organist/bandleader Max McCabe-Lokos, which had earlier exploded into an on-stage fistfight in New York, the band's time together in the cabin sustained the bonds among its members, both musically and personally—at the same time as it enabled them to produce one of the decade's finest albums.

To those who witnessed the band in their early years, the Deadly Snakes in their final era, a decade on, would have presented a startling contrast. For a downtown band that began bristling with adolescent antagonism, who dressed and acted like a retro street gang as a counterpoint to music that ran loose, wild and violent, they seemed unlikely to end their run as refined young men eating, laughing and playing reflective and mournful songs in a rural cabin. Even bound together as they were by a friendship dating back to high school, their internal history was peppered with conflict and violence (including one instance in which three Snakes threw the dictatorial McCabe-Lokos across a hotel room). No one—not even the band—could have predicted the career that would take The Deadly Snakes from the frantic, punk rock and roll of their first LP, *Love Undone*, to the dark, careful pop of their swan song, *Porcella*.

Yet above all, what set the Deadly Snakes apart from the vast majority of their peers—in garage rock, in Canadian popular music in general—was not their ability to grow and change, but their ability to do it well. Many bands make one exciting album before following "new directions" that lead them into wilting self-indulgence, but few start out great and young and wild, and get better as their records grow more challenging and complex. Fewer still have the good sense to recognize that, after having done their best work, the only dignified choice remaining is to disband at the height of their prowess, their friendships intact, maintaining the reputation of a band that never made a weak record.

The Deadly Snakes garnered little attention from the music industry or press in Canada. As Canadian "independent" music was exploding worldwide with the popularity of Montreal's Arcade Fire and Wolf Parade, and Toronto's Feist, Stars and Broken Social Scene, the Deadly Snakes remained largely unknown outside of the garage rock underground they'd outgrown years before. The music industry only formally noticed them a month after they dissolved, when they were nominated for the 2006 Polaris Prize; they declined to reform to play at the ceremony.

McCabe-Lokos says, "My attitude was, 'No! I don't want to bring my organ down there. We broke up!'"

CHAPTER 2

REAL ROCK AND ROLL TONIGHT

"It's a great emotion to base a band on, that arrogant commitment to something that you feel only you know how to do. And it can only be with youth, or you're crazy." – André Ethier

LIKE ALL GREAT rock and roll bands, the Deadly Snakes began in a basement.

Monday nights in high school, the four friends from west end Toronto who would comprise the band's core from beginning to end—McCabe-Lokos, Ethier, Moszynski and gifted trumpet player and multi-instrumentalist Matt "Matt-Dog" Carlson—held a weekly ritual they jokingly called "Boys' Night Out." ("Like we were a bunch of guys hanging out in the garage," laughs McCabe-Lokos.)

Initially, they met in a doughnut shop for coffee and cigarettes, but soon migrated to Ethier's parents' basement, where they could furtively drink. Ethier, who had already begun playing and recording his own music, had instruments lying around, so it made sense that their camaraderie turned musical.

From one basement, the band—initially known as "the Boys Night Out Band"—struck out to another. They made their shaky debut as a four-piece downstairs from a laundromat in Kensington Market during a birthday party for McCabe-Lokos's brother Nick. Having agreed to play the party as a dare to one another, they quickly cobbled together a handful of songs, learned a few covers of bands like the Troggs and steeled themselves to play live for the first time.

"When we played the birthday party," McCabe-Lokos says, "We needed to make up a fake name for our fake band, and decided on *The Deadly Snakes*. The joke was that we had to be, like, a *band*, with a real *band* name. Then the band went on and we were stuck with it."

They chose the name, Ethier recalls, to invoke the image of the sort of gang they might have been in high school in the 50s. The band, he says, was "supposed to be a memory, like something that had already happened."

"We thought that name was really funny," Ethier chuckles ruefully, "when it was only supposed to last a few months."

Chris "Chico" Trowbridge, a former producer of CBC Television's *The Hour* and current producer of CBC Radio-1's *Day 6* with Brent Bambury, was an early mentor to the band, releasing their first 7-inch single on his record label Crazy Money. He was at their debut show in the laundromat where he met the band for the first time. As much as the show was intended to be a joke, for Trowbridge, the introduction was striking.

"So I follow the flyer directions down an alley," he remembers, "down a set of stairs into the basement. There's hardly anybody there, and this little kid, he looked like a 12-year-old, comes up to me and aggressively goes, 'Can I help you?' I tell him I'm there for Nick's birthday, and he says, 'How do you know Nick?' I say, 'I'm a friend from school. He invited me.' That was Max, trying to kick me out of this party that had eight people in it. And he looked like a little boy, like a child. I thought, 'What the fuck is this?'"

When the band finally played, Trowbridge says, "They were borderline terrible—that was one of the great things about the Snakes at the beginning. They were brilliant too—they had written these great songs, these complicated soul ballads, that they could barely play."

Especially striking to Trowbridge was a ballad the band never recorded called "The House of Love," which captured, as much as *Love Undone*'s liner notes eventually would, the band's founding principles. It was, he says, "this sad song about the 'house of love,' and when you go there, you must get married—which was a bad thing! I'm older than those guys, eight or 10 years older, and listening to this I'm wondering, 'What are these little kids doing, singing about getting married?' They were so naïve, but really sophisticated at the same time."

————

Rock and roll has traditionally been the business of young men, and when the Deadly Snakes—all in their teens—formed in 1996, they set out to play music specific to who they were at that time. Three years later, as they released their acclaimed debut *Love Undone*, they used the record's liner notes to state their purpose plainly: the album was "a rally call to abandon irony and play from your soul—to be young and to be bold."

The kind of primal rock and roll the Snakes were playing—high-energy music founded in blues, gospel and R&B—paradoxically remains, over a half-century after it first found its form, the sound of youthful mayhem. Snakes singer/guitarist André Ethier says, "For Max and I and [trumpet player] Matt [Carlson], it was almost evangelical, learning about early rock and roll. We were getting it all at once in this big explosion of soul, gospel, R&B and blues, and I was hearing it with new ears, as *my* music. When you hear Otis Redding for the first time as your own, it's really powerful. We were committed."

There wasn't much rock and roll on the radio in '96, and the way the young Snakes looked at it, rock (*rawwk!*) music was a humiliating disgrace. There was no roll; no one was listening to Little Richard or Otis Redding. "Rock" was at best the domain of guitar shop assholes, at worst the sound of sports bars and Chevy commercials, of the 15-minute-commercial-free-classic-rock-ride soundtrack to being stuck in traffic on the way home from another casual Friday at the office. The genre itself was embarrassing.

"We had this gang mentality," Ethier explains, "where we thought that no one else got it but us, and that really fuelled the band. I now see that as being ridiculous and audacious, but it's a great emotion to base a band on, that arrogant commitment to something that you feel only you know how to do. And it can only be with youth, or you're crazy. When you're 19 it's yours. But, back then, people who'd come around who were older and wanted to behave the same way, I thought that was just insulting. If you respect youth, you give them their space to be young. You behave like your age and be true to your age."

At the time the Deadly Snakes were forming, the Rolling Stones were releasing a spate of late-career albums that the Snakes, collectively, found mortifying. Here were a bunch of 50-something rock stars singing about having lost "my baby" and hanging out with "the drunks and the homeless." Their music had nothing to do with their lives. However, they didn't have a problem with Bob Dylan.

"He's old," says Ethier, "But the records are good, and it's because he's found what's interesting about being old. We took that philosophy to heart, being honest about what our concerns were and trying to find what was interesting about them. Something that's incredibly *un*interesting is hearing people trying to artificially recreate youth when that isn't their lives."

Chris Trowbridge recalls that at the beginning, the Deadly Snakes were "such fucking kids. They had this van they toured in, and if you got into it, it was Burger King wrappers up to your knees and piles and piles of *Archie Digest* comics. They'd spend the tour whiting out the speech bubbles and writing in obscene dialogue."

Trowbridge underlines the fact that, when the band began, Andrew Moszynski "was almost still in that girls-are-icky stage. He was really into cheeseburgers and stuff. Making the world's biggest cheeseburger was something they tried to do. A lot. [In] one of their first interviews, Max made this comment about how all these 30-year-old bands should get off stage and make some room. Andrew was 16 when they were playing gigs, and the rest were right out of high school."

Almost as early as the laundromat debut, Moszynski told Trowbridge ("in utmost seriousness!") that the band had plans for a Deadly Snakes movie.

"It was going to be a full-length feature film," he says, "about how they all cut off their ring-fingers so they could never get married. When I first heard about it, they were trying to figure out how they could fake not having ring fingers."

That, says Trowbridge, captured the essence of the band as a vessel of the young men's friendship. "There was a real boyish constant," he says. "These were people who shared apartments, or slept at each other's places every night—it was very much a gang. Not in a violent way, but like a 50s gang, a group of guys who hung out a lot."

The moniker they'd adopted had a certain power. As the success of the first show made them an actual band that began to write songs and play other shows together, the members of the Snakes developed a collective personality based on the thuggish implication of their name.

"It was supposed to be tongue-in-cheek," McCabe-Lokos admits, "But then we thought, fuck it—we're in Toronto, everyone here's a pussy! Even though we're these skinny middle-class white boys, we might as well be a tough motorcycle band!"

Convinced that they were the only band in existence—or, at least, in Toronto—to channel the spirit of pure rock and roll, they were soon wearing matching denim jackets with their names and Deadly Snakes patches on the back. Band members spent all their time together and travelled as a group.

Their shows attracted chaos. "Even before I joined the band, I used to go see them play in the first few years, and there was always a lot of broken glass," says saxophonist Jeremi Madsen. "I remember one show in particular at the Lion's Club, this old bar up on College, where people were peeing in the pockets of the pool table, and peeing in the plants, the urinal was ripped off the wall, and the whole place was littered in broken glass."

Simon Harvey, who runs Toronto-based all-vinyl record label Ugly Pop, says that the band was one of the most exciting in the city: "That was at a time when punk rock and hardcore had gotten really tired. Garage rock in general, and the Deadly Snakes in particular, had the kind of energy that hardcore punk used to have, which is why a lot of the older people who'd been into punk gravitated toward them."

Toronto's infamous promoter Dan Burke concurs, claiming that he owes his career in promotion to the draw of their talent. "The Deadly Snakes were a fuckin' machine," he says, "almost a genre unto themselves. They were of unparalleled importance to the live music scene in this city for 10 years." Burke is effusive in his gratitude to the Snakes. "They were a cornerstone of everything I did," he says. "They were a band where not only were their own shows great, but the fact that they were with me gave me morale to carry on."

Explaining what made the Snakes so powerful, Burke says, "What you look for in the form [of rock and roll] is some kind of intelligence, and passion and desire. These exceptional young men are true to the form."

"At the beginning," says Ethier, "there was a band personality that we took on, so we'd see each other in that personality. We'd go out—not consciously, but we'd go out as 'The Deadly Snakes.' We cultivated this weird gang persona."

Ethier, original Snakes saxophonist Carson Binks, and Max McCabe-Lokos's brother Nick moved into a storefront on Bathurst Street, which they treated as the band/gang clubhouse, painting the walls red and the floors black and mounting a framed picture of Hells Angels beating hippies at Altamont on the wall. In the front window they displayed a copy of their debut single "Real Rock & Roll Tonight" flanked by two air rifles. From that entrenched position they cultivated rivalries with other bands they felt were somehow untrue to rock and roll.

One rivalry, with Toronto band Danko Jones, came about by accident.

"We did an interview with Arish [Khan][4] from Montreal garage punk band the Spaceshits for *Vice*, back when it was newsprint," Ethier remembers. "In that interview we made fun of [Hamilton indie record label] Sonic Unyon ads that were all about 'rock and roll.' We didn't know Danko Jones had just signed with them, and we were saying that it wasn't a real rock and roll label. *Vice* didn't want to print it because Sonic Unyon was one of their only advertisers at the time. We found out later that the guys from Danko Jones thought we were making reference to them."

Because their friends in the Spaceshits had a rivalry with Tricky Woo, Ethier says, "We just agreed with them. And also, Max ended up dating the girlfriend of the singer from Tricky

---

4 Now better known as King Khan, of King Khan and the Shrines. Since 2002, he has played and recorded off and on with former Spaceshits frontman Mark "BBQ" Sultan as the King Khan and BBQ Show.

Woo after they broke up, and he wasn't really into that."

They also managed to nurture a rivalry with Toronto band the Killer Elite, of which Snakes drummer Andrew Moszynski and sax player Carson Binks were actually members (along with comedian Nick Flanagan, later frontman of the beloved hardcore-punk/comedy group the Brutal Knights).

"Mike [Gribben], the singer of [the Killer Elite], hated us, I guess because he was sharing members with us," Ethier remembers. "They were on the cover of *Now* magazine, and he made a point of saying in the interview that they were better than the Snakes, and we weren't real, while they were the real deal."

As a result of the incessant drama and legends of rivalry, the Deadly Snakes became known as a band that fought with other groups.

"I remember a guy who was in another band coming up to us when we were out and saying, 'We should start a fake rivalry for the press,'" Ethier recounts shamefacedly. "And we said, 'No, let's start a real rivalry, right now' and threatened him. We were assholes, arrogant assholes." After a moment of reflection, he adds, "I don't even think they were a band that played more than a couple of shows. It would have been a lame rivalry, anyway."

Yet the arrogance and antagonism masked the real bond among the Snakes. Like their spiritual forbears the Ramones, the Snakes' allegiance was founded from the beginning on close, deep camaraderie, and that friendship would remain the core value of the band. While they deliberately wrote songs that celebrated people and places in Toronto's west end, they also sought to deter outsiders from their circle.

McCabe-Lokos, in particular, developed a reputation for defending early Snakes shows from outsiders, occasionally to the point of absurdity. Remembering his surly reception of Trowbridge at the laundromat, Ethier says, "I don't know if it was because he thought [Trowbridge] was too old, but he'd just deny people access if he didn't know them."

Ethier recalls a similar incident at another of the birthday parties the Snakes played in their infancy.

"He was doing door, but it was a free show!" Ethier laughs. "I guess he was policing. Carson, the original sax player, ended up blowing up at him. He went up to the door just as Max was barring these four hot girls from coming in because he didn't know them. Carson's reaction was, 'What the hell are you doing? This is the point of everything!'"

"The mentality Max had," says Trowbridge, "was 'This is *our* thing, and it has to be protected.'"

CHAPTER 3

SO YOUNG AND SO CRUEL

"I'm a fucking cabaret, man." – Max McCabe-Lokos

MAX MCCABE-LOKOS is small in stature and enormous in personality. When we meet at the Rhino in Toronto's Parkdale neighbourhood, around which he and the rest of the Snakes grew up and which they memorialize in many of their songs, his entrance is quiet but striking. He's wearing a leather jacket, a tweed flat cap, a light scarf tied around his neck, and has a tidy English-style moustache. This look straddles the line between debonair and ridiculous without ever touching down on either side: he could be a French airman, or Snoopy's brother Spike, but he's neither. When he sits down to talk, his manner is both commanding and self-conscious: he's used to having the floor and he's comfortable with it, but there's something about him that says he's nervous he might lose his position.

In conversation, McCabe-Lokos is warm and candid and very engaging: he has a fidgety double-espresso energy that's infectious even as it reveals how tightly he's wound.

He's easy to describe as a "character," and while if he were a teenager he might seem like he was trying too hard, at 30, the combination of the suave and the outrageous seems perfectly natural.

These days, McCabe-Lokos is a character actor playing small-to-medium sized parts in feature films like *The Incredible Hulk*, *Lars and the Real Girl*, *Max Payne* and George Romero's *Land of the Dead*, in which he plays a skateboarding miscreant eventually eaten by zombies. In 2010 he had a recurring role on the short-lived ABC drama *Happy Town*; the same year, he wrote, produced, directed and starred in the short film *Paris 1919*. As of August of 2012, he is working on financing his first feature film. This career direction comes as a surprise to no one who knows him, and McCabe-Lokos admits that it suits him well.

An old acquaintance remembers her first impression of McCabe-Lokos in high school: spurned at a party by a girl he'd had a crush on for some time, McCabe-Lokos dealt with rejection by climbing dramatically out onto the fire escape into the pouring rain with a bottle of Baby Duck. There he remained, wretched and drenched and drunk, for the rest of the night.

I carefully repeat the anecdote to McCabe-Lokos, worried it'll embarrass or offend him, but he only laughs self-effacingly and shakes his head. "I'm a fucking cabaret, man," he explains with a sheepish shrug. "I'm a big personality, and that's as far as I'll go with that." This is an understatement: notorious for on-stage antics that have included stripping his clothes off, standing on his organ, and loudly belittling other Snakes, McCabe-Lokos's stage presence defined the

Snakes' live shows.

Especially as time went on, the Deadly Snakes belonged to every one of its members: all were exceptional musicians able to assert themselves creatively, and the music they produced profited from the pooling of their contributions. Yet, in many ways, the Snakes were McCabe-Lokos's band, a statement each member echoes in one way or another.

"I made it my business to be the boss of the band," he explains, "even if it was only in my imagination—which I don't think it was. I'm kind of a control freak. If I think I'm doing something for the good of other people, for the greater good, then that justifies it. I guess I should just relax."

"Max was the driving force in the band," says Ethier, "and even though everyone's musical tastes were combined to make the band, I feel like the general aesthetic from the beginning was always based on him. If the music of the Snakes ever represented one person, it was Max. He's the heart of the band."

As the Snakes' captain, McCabe-Lokos exerted his authority at times by taking on and getting done all the hard work himself, and at other times by intimidating and bullying the other band members.

"Max is an A-type personality," Ethier explains, "and he wants or needs to be in charge—and he should be, because he's really good at being in charge."

"But to be totally honest," he continues, "a lot of the conflict in the band came about because Max, when we started, saw me as a songwriter. I'd been in bands before and was already writing and singing, so I was to be the singer of the band and write songs. But it was to be a band that represented Max, in a sense, so a lot of the conflict came from him needing me to write songs but wanting me to write the songs that he would write if he could write songs himself. There was a lot of push and pull about power. It was ultimately Max's band—Max had started the band with Andrew, and they invited me. So he was trying to write the songs through me, but *I* had to write the songs."

That the Snakes formed at such an early age, all agree, did not encourage the development of healthy and mature relationships.

"When we started," McCabe-Lokos says, "I was 18, and when you establish those rules at that age, then—it's like, if you have one childhood friend, and you have this particular relationship with that person. Certain jokes come out, or a side of you that's different—all these things that are fixed in childhood. And things that are formed in childhood, then that's your reference for it. When we were 18 and I was parading around like the boss, then I was always the boss after that, in that setting, and Andrew was the comedy, and Matt was the quiet one. It got to a point that after 10 years, these roles were so fucking etched out that they weren't representations of real personalities anymore, they were just representations of people's personalities in *that setting*. Which is almost satirical."

At the beginning of the band, Ethier says, "Max had just started working for his dad, who's a foreman at a pretty serious construction company. He was working with guys who solved problems by shouting at each other on the job. Because he was new and young, he caught a lot of shit at work, and it was really stressful for him. That stress came out in the context of our band because there, he was able to dominate. That's all from the very beginning of the band—Andrew was 16, I was 19, and those are relationships that you develop when you're 18 or 19. But the problem was that it established a power structure and a way of dealing with problems that continued all the way through our twenties. Everyone had grown up, and they were living mature lives outside of the band, but every time we had to go back to the band, we had this really immature way of dealing with problems."

"I was so involved in the Deadly Snakes," Max says, "that even if I didn't write all the songs, I was totally the Stalin figure in that little group."

Yet as much as McCabe-Lokos's manner was a source of frequent tension, it was also an uncomfortable catalyst. Chris Trowbridge remembers how central the power struggle and tensions were to the band's accomplishments.

"Max is a forceful guy, you know," he says, "and there was a lot of tension in the band. The thing was, there was tension, but they spent every waking minute together. Max had the same role in the Snakes that Johnny Ramone had in the Ramones: if he was the Stalin of the band, he was leading people who were *highly* undisciplined and actively difficult to work with. Everyone was so passive aggressive, and Max was an asshole. He was really difficult and drove everybody crazy even as he was trying to get people off their asses. He didn't do it the right way, and the decisions he tried to push through weren't always the right things, so there was resistance with good reason. But he's a really good guy, and a really sweet guy too."

———

André Ethier is in many ways a stark contrast to McCabe-Lokos. Tall and slim with a strong, resonant voice that contrasts McCabe-Lokos's controlled timbre, Ethier has the placid ease of an old-timer in a spaghetti western. His manner is so laid back it's almost sleepy, but in conversation he's deep and thoughtful. It's not that he isn't paying attention, but just that he doesn't get agitated over much.

More than any other former Snake, Ethier gives the first impression of being very much an adult. All the Snakes—now well past 30—are mature and thoughtful, but Ethier in particular effortlessly wears the role of a grown man. Partly due to his appearance—mostly bald on top, he's compensated with the kind of woolly beard popular in the early 80s with his generation's fathers. He speaks with quiet candour, drifting gently into each topic. Like McCabe-Lokos, Ethier has carved out a serious artistic career for himself. Early showings of his paintings received attention from the *New York Times*, and he has since been written up in the *Village Voice*, the *New Yorker* and many more publications for his solo exhibitions across Canada, Europe, the U.S. and Japan.

"I'm reasonably successful," he says, "even if I'm not hugely successful. The economic collapse was hard on the whole art business, but things are alright."

Ethier supplements his income with work as a tech in the Education Department of the Art Gallery of Ontario. As well, he maintains a solo career as a singer-songwriter and has released four mostly acoustic albums.

Like McCabe-Lokos, he too wears a tweed flat-cap. Unlike McCabe-Lokos, however, he doesn't wear it so much with flair as with inevitability. When I met him for the first time over toast and tea at The Beaver cafe on Queen West, he told me that he and his wife Kai were expecting their first child shortly; today, their son Louis is four years old. ("He's a good boy," says Ethier.) André and Kai went to the once-reviled "House of Love" in the fall of 2005, just after the Snakes returned from recording *Porcella* in the cabin.

"To a lot of people, living with your girlfriend and being married—these are things that our generation avoids," he explains with easy care. "There are a lot of 30-somethings behaving like 20-year-olds. I think that's gross; it's wasteful. People who are afraid of commitment—that makes me think they're afraid of life. Responsibilities, like having a child and a house, are things that help you become more yourself and help you to flourish. People who think that responsibility means you're growing up, and growing up is something to be avoided, I think they're missing out on a big part of what's enjoyable about life. But it's a much subtler taste."

As he's explaining this, I find it hard not to reflect that nine years earlier, he and the Snakes were recording "I Gotta Plan (For Saturday Night)" for their debut record. That rowdy party stomp—anchored to Ethier's holler, "I gotta plan for Saturday night: Get drunk! Basketball! Go crazy down by the school!"—might as well have been a thesis statement for the work of the early Snakes. It was a concise declaration of their intent: to create loud, drunken rock and roll meant to be enjoyed in an honest shirt-drenched sweat with friends, reeling together in the delight of being young.

Because he seems so naturally adult, Ethier is the hardest of the Deadly Snakes to imagine as a teenager. McCabe-Lokos is—like most people—easy to picture young because you can imagine him being sort of the same, fervent and jittery, minus those elements of maturity that are the by-products of passing time: his poise, his reflection and the timing of his wit. Ethier, however, is so smoothly imperturbable that it's difficult to picture him an inelegant youth—though the cover photo of *Love Undone*, on which he peeks out from behind the scrum of the band with a gap-toothed Alfred E. Newman grin, disturbs that presumption.

Even at the beginning, however, the youthful audaciousness of the Snakes wasn't a direct expression of Ethier's personality. Prior to forming the Snakes, he had already begun writing and performing his own songs, which he remembers were "more musically advanced than the Snakes, or at least more interesting lyrically." But as the group of friends, in the band's early days, adopted a collective-personality based on their name and appearance, Ethier found it necessary to write songs from the perspective of that image, purposefully dumbing down the music and the lyrics.

"It was a difficult balance," he says, "but an exciting one. The lyrics still needed to have meaning and resonance, but you had to be so casual about it, as if it had just occurred to you. It had to sound really natural, like the lyrics were happening immediately."

Part of what fuelled the early songwriting was the desire to embrace their age. "We weren't idiots. We knew about the image of a youthful, wild band," says McCabe-Lokos. "We were younger than most bands, but in our heads, that was the age you were supposed to be in a band. So we played it up. We didn't actually live, like, 'get drunk, basketball, go crazy down by the school.' You're playing to the images."

"I always thought of the *Deadly Snakes* as an entity being a lot like Eddie from Iron Maiden," Ethier explains, referring to that band's ubiquitous zombie/ghoul mascot, "this monster that we'd created to represent us. But I think I imagined it into existence. The whole writing process for the Snakes was me in a relationship with *The Deadly Snakes*—capital T. D. S.—and what I imagined us to be. It's weird because it must mean that I'd removed myself from it and saw myself as separate. I wrote to that imagined personality."

The vast majority of the conflict in the band was between Ethier and McCabe-Lokos. And while the source of friction was often obvious, at least some of it came from their images of each other. Ethier wrote songs to fit with the persona he figured McCabe-Lokos wanted for the band, but he was surprised to discover McCabe-Lokos's songs, when he began writing them, were more concerned with storytelling and character than Ethier's celebrations of good times, frustrations and attitude.

Ethier is an inveterate nice guy; he was the last of the Snakes whom I met, and each one who preceded him correctly predicted I would like him immediately, saying, "He's the most easygoing guy you'll ever meet." But if McCabe-Lokos's energy could turn into shouted orders, thrown objects and threats, Ethier's serenity could equally become a destructive passivity, even in the absence of actual pressure from band members.

"This is so ridiculous," he says. "But: I have a beard. I like to grow my beard—I don't know why. I feel connected with it. But I always felt that I shouldn't have a beard in the band, so I'd have to shave my beard every time we went on tour or played a show. That was my thing—no one in the band ever asked me to shave my beard. It was my concept of the band that wouldn't allow me to have a beard on stage."

I recall seeing pictures of McCabe-Lokos playing shows with a moustache, and Ethier replies with a shrug, "Yeah, sometimes he'd grow a beard, even."

"I'd say," he deliberates, "that I see The Deadly Snakes—capital T. D. S.—as its own entity, and the personalities within it are my friends when they're in the Snakes. The Snakes has its own personality, whereas Andrew as an individual, and Max as individual—they're different. I have my feelings for Max, who's a great guy. That's just Max and me. Then there's Max in the band, and if I discuss that, it brings up other feelings. But that's Max-in-the-band. All of them—it's them in the context of this entity."

CHAPTER 4

LOVE UNDONE

"We were just all on the same page musically, all
suckers for old dirty soul." – Andrew Moszynski

SUCCESS, IN THE SHAPE that they pursued it, came quickly for
the Snakes. The band was only supposed to last until the end of
the summer of '96, when Ethier moved to Montreal to start art
school, but it was too much fun to quit, and Ethier frequently
returned home to practice and play shows with the band.

"Montreal's a beautiful city to be lonely in," he reflects,
"but I remember being sad and wanting always to be home.
I was pretty much still in Toronto, but sleeping in Montreal."

One of the band's first fans was Jay Ferguson, of power-
pop powerhouse Sloan, who saw one of the first Snakes
shows and insisted they join Sloan on a Canadian tour. As a
result, the Snakes played their fourth gig after the laundromat basement in Toronto's Varsity Arena.

"Even when they were opening for Sloan," says Chris
Trowbridge, "they were really creaky. They'd almost fall
apart. But people with good taste in music, people like Jay

Ferguson, really loved them, because they were just a real, organic band. And they were so bad, but they acted like they were the Rolling Stones, which was really charming."

Early on, the Snakes saw Montreal's hell-raising garage punks the Spaceshits play in-store at Toronto's Rotate This! record shop and spent the afternoon with the band, digging for records and playing dice in a parking lot. The two bands formed an alliance that would be central to the Snakes' development.

"We knew immediately that they were on the same page as us," Andrew Moszynski says. "They were all basically the same age, and they, more than anyone else, turned the Snakes into a real band. They said, 'We're gonna go on tour, and we're taking you with us. And we're gonna call [influential garage punk record label] Sympathy [for the Record Industry] and make sure they put out your first record.' The Spaceshits are the greatest guys. They're so instrumental to sending the Snakes along the path of not just being a one-off party band."

Within a couple of years, the Snakes had begun to play out of town and make a name for themselves in the North American garage punk underground even as they cultivated a following in Toronto with their defiantly local songs.

Says Ethier, "We recognized—at Chris Trowbridge's suggestion, actually—that you become more universal in your songwriting through being specific. We were talking about early Van Morrison songs that mentioned street names, and that led to trying to be specific to our experience."

"If you say, 'I'm going down to Kensington Market,'" Trowbridge says, "even if you don't know where the fuck Kensington Market is, it's a better thing than saying, 'I'm going downtown.'"

Far from expressing Toronto pride, the Snakes intended their songs to reflect Toronto as a necessary backdrop. "None of us would actually *celebrate* Toronto," Ethier explains. "I love my home, and I love being home, but we wrote about Toronto not because Toronto is interesting or a good city. It just happens to be where we're from."

They also continued to play small shows and parties, like birthdays for Nick McCabe-Lokos that were sequels to the laundromat show.

"Those shows were always the best," says Ethier. "Crazy, fun, no one wearing shirts, then everyone would go swimming afterwards. It was always the first really warm weekend of the summer, at the end of June." Following the second birthday show, Moszynski badly cut his hand jumping a fence while running from police after the group was caught swimming illegally; Ethier remembers him playing shows proudly wearing the blood-stained T-shirt with which he'd bandaged his hand. The birthday gigs were so formative to the band that they eventually memorialized the atmosphere of drunken chaos and illegal night swimming in the 2003 video for "I Can't Sleep at Night."

True to their word, the Spaceshits began to take the Deadly Snakes with them on tours across the U.S. Moszynski was still in high school.

"I'd come back to school in September and everyone would trade stories about what they did during the summer," he remembers. "Everyone else would be saying, 'Yeah, I played video games with so-and-so,' while meanwhile I could say, 'I went down to New Orleans with my five best friends in the world. We lived in a van for two weeks and behaved like idiots.'"

In the course of touring, they met Greg ("Greg Oblivian") Cartwright, of Memphis garage punk figureheads the Oblivians (and today of the critically-acclaimed group Reigning Sound). Known for leading fierce rock and roll bands fuelled by the same high-test R&B as the Snakes, Cartwright was, Chris Trowbridge says, "probably one of the only living musicians under the age of 60 that the Snakes respected."

"The Oblivians were leaps and bounds better than every other garage band," says Moszynski, "because they weren't listening to other garage bands. They listened to everything. You could tell they had incredible record collections: soul, country, a little bit of everything that's good. They wrote the songs they wanted in the style they wanted, and that's what made them the greatest band of that whole scene."

Previously, Cartwright had fronted the Compulsive Gamblers. The Deadly Snakes, Ethier declares, "existed because of the Gamblers. When we started, we wanted to be the Compulsive Gamblers. That was the exact genre that we wanted to play."

After opening for the Oblivians at Toronto's Horseshoe Tavern, the Snakes put them up at Moszynski's parents' house.

"We stayed up all night drinking on the porch, hanging out with our favourite band," Moszynski says. "Then we went down to Memphis about two months later with the Spaceshits and ended up staying with Greg. He said, 'Listen, if you get together to make a record, just fly me up and I'll be the producer. I'd love to do it.' It was as easy as that. We were just all on the same page musically, all suckers for old dirty soul."

That was how Cartwright came to produce *Love Undone*,

recorded in three days during the record-breaking blizzard of January 1999, a storm so bad that Toronto Mayor Mel Lastman famously called in the army to help in the snow-removal efforts.

Despite anomalous bands like the Oblivians, by the end of the 90s the garage rock underground had become tedious and self-parodying. Too many bands—tattoo-spackled and attitude-copping—played with too little inspiration, re-enacting 60s garage rock without the youthful energy of the genre's original players or the interest in the primarily black music (R&B, gospel, blues) that inspired them.

"There were a million bands that only listened to the other 10 garage bands on their record label," Moszynski laughs. "That's just the same sort of recycled sound. But there's a reason the Sonics played all those songs—so *you* wouldn't have to."

As a result, *Love Undone* came as a delightful shock to many. Wild, fresh and loud, the Deadly Snakes cut away the bulky affectations of the genre to produce music that was lean, swift, and, above all, a lot of fun. The record wanted listeners to play it loud and fly off the handle dancing to it. You're supposed to bump into people, knock things over, break stuff, get some-one's drink down your shirt and wear it all with a grin—because it sounds *that* good.

From the cacophony of drums and cymbals, guitar and smashed piano that begins "Bone Dry," the album's two-chord opener, to the arrival of a horn section for once used (as horns should be) to punctuate and underline, *Love Undone* sets out from the first in pursuit of a good time. But it's the second song, the album's title track, that lays out the record's theme, to which each subsequent song will return, in different ways and from different angles. The torrent of guitar, harmonica and drums that open "Love Undone" like a fire hose of sound tumble into verses defined by a drum line of loosely rocking rolls, around which guitar and harmonica and saxophone circle each other, occasionally colliding in feedback. The attitude of the capital T. D. S. Snakes is all over the record, from the adolescent fervour of "I Gotta Plan (For Saturday Night)" to the hometown lament "I Don't Wanna Have to Hate This City" to the I'm-going-to-literally-murder-that-guy-if-you-don't-stop-going-out-with-him slowdance "Cotton Stained Red" (the latter recalling more than anything the early, bluesy *Bang! Sessions* recordings by Van Morrison beloved by the Snakes).

It's hard, listening to music so hot and good, not to want to be at the front of a room full of friends losing their minds while the band gives everything they've got to make sure they, and you, together, have a fantastic time. That's what the album is about, after all. As the liner notes explain, the 12 songs that compose *Love Undone* "reflect the loyalties, grudges, wild nights, and heartbreaks of six longtime friends." It's natural, listening to this album, to think of your own friends, because it's good time music, and who would you rather have beside you for the good times?

The sound of *Love Undone* is hard to name; the gruff production makes it essentially a "lo-fi" album, but not in the sense that it's played lazily like so many records of that subgenre. It sounds, rather, like it was recorded on ancient equipment that it totally overwhelmed, but the extent to which it surpasses its recording technology is also a measure of its exhilaration. Like all subsequent Snakes records, *Love Undone* features no obvious instrument effects and a minimum of production interference. It was recorded almost entirely live as the band sought to plainly capture what they sounded like as a group, playing their instruments together in a room.

Their "we-are-what-we-are" stance is reflected in the album's cover photo, a hideous portrait of the band, mouths hanging open, looking gawky and unhealthy.

"I don't know what the fuck we were thinking," laughs Moszynski when I bring up the photo. "We were just the kings of settling on things. You know, 'That's good enough, we look like mutants. Let's make that our first offering to the world.' I guess we didn't know any photographers. That was just a timer picture, everyone standing in this corner of Max's apartment. Maybe we only had a few shots on the last roll of film? We must have known someone with a camera at that point, but we just never made the call."

To an outsider, though, the photo's unsightliness seems to suggest they were too busy playing music to pose for a retake, or too confident in the quality of the record to bother tidying up its cover. *Love Undone*, typical of the Snakes, passes unspoken judgment on the rest of the music industry by suggesting that careful production and pretty packaging— later excruciatingly posed covers by the Mooney Suzuki and the Black Halos come to mind—are the refuge of those who can't play well enough to sell their product straight.

"[Punk bible] *Maximumrockandroll* reviewed the album," says Moszynski, "and called us something like, 'A large, ugly band that must get laid all the time if they play like this.' If that's what it takes to end up in *Maximumrockandroll*, sacrificing my reputation as a normal looking guy, I'll go with that."

———————

Adulation for *Love Undone* was immediate—it turned up on most garage rock critic's top 10 and best of the year lists, as rumour of the band's raucous live shows spread. That process was helped in large part by the record's coming out, thanks to the Spaceshits, on L.A.'s influential Sympathy for the Record Industry label (best known for breaking the White Stripes, whose debut the label released a month or two later). Because they had an American label, the Snakes toured mostly in the U.S., where their youthful excitement was unusual and unexpected.

"We thought that garage rock was supposed to be youth-based," says Ethier, "because that's what the scene was like in Toronto. But I think we actually got it wrong, because we were so far removed from the American culture that produced garage rock. When we got down to the States and started playing shows, we were shocked by how old everyone actually was. The crowd was all record collectors in their 30s. Now that I'm closer to that age, I understand it, but when we were first faced with that we just hated garage. It wasn't the scene we expected it to be. We wanted out."

Though the Snakes recoiled, they kept touring for the adventure of it. They were young and touring meant the opportunity to scroll the continent in the company of their best friends. As Chad Ross, who became the Snakes' bassist prior to their third album, points out, the Snakes existed in a pre-iPod, pre-laptop culture of touring. Ross, who has toured as a guitar tech with Vancouver psych rock favourites Black Mountain, laments that most bands on the road these days retire to listen to music or watch movies with headphones in the van.

When the Snakes toured, though, they amused themselves constantly as a group. They invented van games ("What Kind of Soda is My Finger?"—in which, Ethier says "You would whisper the name of the soda while pretending to drink from your finger"—along with "What Kind of Hat is My Finger?" and "Where in the World is My Finger?") and van riddles ("Q: What is the world's tallest free-standing flower? A: The CN Flower"), and wrote one-page scripts that they filmed in the van as they drove. Touring, therefore, was an extension of the Bathurst St. clubhouse that they could take anywhere.

In the period of touring that followed *Love Undone*'s release, Greg Cartwright contacted the band.

"He had some time on his hands," says Moszynski. "So he called us up and said, 'Hey, can I tag along on your tour and just play second guitar for you?' We said, 'Fucking absolutely!' The Oblivians and the Compulsive Gamblers are our favourite bands and he's a great guy to hang around—get in the van! During that tour he laid it out and said, 'Listen, there's no one else I want to play with. I want to be in this band.' So we said, 'We'll make it work like the Band did! You can be our Levon Helm!'"

At the time, other shifts in Snakes membership were taking place: original saxophone player Carson Binks left and was replaced by Jeremi Madsen, an old friend of most of the band.

"Someone had mentioned he played in high school," Ethier says, "and we asked him if he could play in our band.

The only notes he knows how to play on the saxophone are ones from Snakes stuff. He's not really a sax player—he can play bass and guitar. He's not a non-musician, but he only played sax in the Snakes. I don't think he had any interest in playing saxophone at all. Also, Carson, the first saxophone player, plays bass now. None of our sax players ever really wanted to play sax, or liked the sax."

Original bassist Yuri Didrichson, who had been replaced by James Sayce before the recording of *Love Undone*, returned for the recording of the band's second album before later quitting again—he was replaced by a guy named Randy for the subsequent tour. Adding Greg Cartwright—something of an idol, who had spent most of the decade he had on the band members touring the same circuit they were now playing—seemed like a pretty safe investment.

Ethier remembers, "We went on this tour [of the U.S.] where we backed him up on his songs, and then he played in the band instead of just sitting on the side of the stage. And it was the best tour we ever did. It was my favourite, anyway. So I understand why after that, naturally, we'd say to ourselves that we should have him in the band. But I remember thinking that was a bad idea, that we'd pushed our admiration of Greg into a place where it shouldn't go, where it's not actually beneficial but it seems exciting."

CHAPTER 5

I'M NOT YOUR SOLDIER ANYMORE

"It was crazy. But it turns out you can pull off a really
good show even after puking into your hands."
– Andrew Moszynski

CARTWRIGHT'S MEMBERSHIP in the band proved to be more
complex than expected, and he joined the Snakes at a point
of uneasy development. From the beginning, Ethier had
been the lead singer and, though most of the songs were
crafted together by the group, he tended to bring more song
ideas and lyrics to the table than anyone else. This inspired a
certain tension in the band's performances stemming from
McCabe-Lokos's desire to display his command.

"Max knew," says Ethier, "that because I was singing,
people would perceive me to be the main guy in the band,
so a lot of his performance, earlier on, was in conflict with
me because he wanted to be seen as co-main guy."

"The band was always sort of me and André who were
the show," McCabe-Lokos says. Then he stops and corrects
himself. "*Everybody* was, the whole band, for sure, but in

the beginning *I thought* I was what the room was looking at. They may not have been! But in my mind they were, and I would try to put on a show with the organ."

"I felt undermined," Ethier says, "because often, right before going on stage, he'd tell me, 'Don't say anything,' and just pull the carpet out from under me. He'd say a bunch of stuff to me, and I'd get uncomfortable, then he'd get really crazy on stage—taking his pants off and standing on his organ, that kind of thing. It kind of suited me, though—it's more in keeping with my personality to be quiet on stage. Anyway, I do think that's where the conflict started—he wanted to start a band but didn't write songs or sing, so he needed me, and then I think he resented me for being the one who did write the songs."

Cartwright managed to enter the group as McCabe-Lokos was beginning to work his way toward frontman status by writing and singing more. And though the Snakes were strongly influenced by the Band—especially their earlier incarnation the Hawks, who backed Bob Dylan on his controversial early electric tours—Cartwright turned out to fall less into the Levon Helm role they'd envisioned and more into that of a Dylan figure. He was older, more accomplished and a natural focal point.

"Greg was supposed to be a guitar player," says McCabe-Lokos, "and he started stealing the show. He's a fucking great performer, and it's not something I think he did on purpose, but that made him the de facto frontman—of a band that already had one and a half frontmen. So I was like, who's this guy who just comes in, starts playing guitar, and then suddenly we're getting billed as 'The Deadly Snakes –

Featuring Greg Oblivian!' or 'Greg Oblivian and the Deadly Snakes.' We were *a band* before him, and *after* him."

Cartwright, reached by phone at his home in North Carolina, says, "The Deadly Snakes was Max's band, and it meant all the world to him. I think it was terrifying to him to think that someone else's vision could take over the band. Which it obviously wasn't going to, but I understand why he felt that way."

Cartwright recalls feeling that McCabe-Lokos was challenging him constantly over trivial matters to maintain his status as the band's principal decision maker.

"As I would bring it up with other members," he says, "their response was that he'd always been that way, and that he had a Napoleon complex. They let him act that way because they loved him—which I understood as well. But it does take a toll over time. And I was a newcomer, had not known him all my life, and I was not prepared to put up with temper tantrums. It was a very bizarre thing to land in."

The addition of Cartwright to the Snakes increased the band's already considerable internal tensions. During the recording of *Love Undone*, Ethier says, "we had a really happy relationship—that whole record was so happy for us, and we were so happy to have him there. Then as soon as he officially joined, it disrupted the balance of how the Snakes worked. Because Max couldn't control Greg. Greg was older than him."

"I had more of a power struggle with that guy than André," says McCabe-Lokos. "André's really easygoing, but with Greg, that was different. We had real fights—we were in each other's faces. Him in his own passive-aggressive way, and me in a very audible way. He's a bit more seasoned and experienced, so I think he sort of wanted us to know it. We'd go on tour, and he would always sit in the front. There was no question. He was kind of a baby. When he wanted something, he got it. Like, he always drove, even though it was my van. I remember he once tried to rationalize that—that he was older and had more experience. It wasn't a good argument."

"What Max probably doesn't know," Ethier reports with some reticence, "is that Greg talked to us and said, 'Listen, I'm probably going to drive a lot on this tour, because I don't trust Max's driving.' Max had just gotten his driver's license and was a very aggressive driver. I'm sure he's a great driver now, but back then he was a new driver at a time when we were doing a lot of drives. So Greg said he didn't trust his driving and asked us to let him do the driving, and I think that made Max feel emasculated."

Cartwright went from a supporting role to a member of the Snakes in time for the recording of their second record. Mc-Cabe-Lokos was, on that album, testing his strength as a singer: he shared lead vocals with Ethier on two tracks and, for the first time, took the lead on his own song "Pirate Cowboy" (a fine and surprisingly light-hearted number blending Toronto regionalism with gay-party-pirate iconography—smartly summed up in the line, "I was born in Parkdale, but my heart is in Penzance"). Cartwright might have fit more easily into the band had he participated in the slow process of writing songs as a group, but instead he arrived from Memphis with a collection of finished numbers for the Snakes to learn.

"What makes it such a bad record, in my opinion," says McCabe-Lokos, "is that he wrote a bunch of stuff in Memphis, we wrote a bunch of stuff the way we always did, together in Toronto, and then he came to Toronto, and we'd learn [his songs]. We didn't all write songs together, which is why it doesn't sound like a cohesive record."

"His songs didn't drop into the mix as well as maybe I'd hoped," Moszynski says. "That wasn't the way that we worked, where you'd sit down and let the song grow. He'd just sort of pop in and go, 'Here's the verse, here's the chorus, repeat three times.'"

"Those aren't Snakes songs," Ethier says flatly. "They're really just Greg's songs. He taught them to us and we played them."

The resulting album, *I'm Not Your Soldier Anymore* (released on L.A.'s In the Red Records, who remained the Snakes' label until they broke up), is patchy and easy to dismiss as a sophomore slump record. Critically, however, it was received as well as its predecessor, if not more so because Cartwright's involvement made the Snakes a garage-punk supergroup. Almost all the songs on the album are strong, but don't have much in common with one another and consequently don't sound like they belong together. Cartwright sings his numbers with his trademarked seething-nutjob delivery and the Snakes trek through the songs behind him, hardly opening up the way they do with their own material. The very impulse to differentiate between "their songs" and "Cartwright's songs"—an easy distinction to make, even among fans of the record, of the Snakes and of Cartwright—is a sign of the album's weakness.

Also strange is the album's finale, "Say Hello," a strong country ballad that builds slowly to a soulful chorus that's just reaching a howling climax when it abruptly fades to silence. It's clearly not over, but it ends there anyway, its premature finish awkward and wanting. I ask Ethier why they recorded it that way and he laughs.

"That wasn't the end," he says. "The song went on, but what happened is: there's this button on a mixing board that shouldn't exist. What it does, if you press it, is it erases everything after that point. And the guy we had recording the album liked to smoke a lot of hash. We'd recorded the track and were playing it back, when the engineer somehow slipped and pressed that button, meaning we lost a good section of the song. We could have gone back and rerecorded it, but by that point time was tight, so we had to settle for fading it out."

And then there's the evident personal friction of the album. It's not audible, but it's clear if you're listening closely. McCabe-Lokos is emerging into the spotlight of the band, and his voice—more frenzied than Ethier's in style and delivery—forges new ground as Snakes' territory, introducing humour, dramatic monologue and a sardonic tone that deliberately contrasts Ethier's sweat-soaked earnestness. These two voices pulling against one another create an appealing creative tension, but Cartwright's songs pull elsewhere and the record chafes against itself. It has the awkwardness of growing up, particularly that point in later adolescence when you know you're ready to take on greater responsibilities but don't yet know how to do that. The discomfort extends to the name of the album.

Ethier says, "We didn't have a title; then Max decided that he wanted it to be called *I'm Not Your Soldier Anymore*, because he had misheard lyrics in a gospel song that sounded like that and thought that it was poetic. Greg hated that title because he thought it was pretentious and he didn't know what it meant. He said something like, 'I didn't write any songs to that type of title.' I bet you he didn't like it because Compulsive Gamblers had broken up and the Oblivians had broken up only recently before, and he didn't want it to be him on the cover of this record as though it was pointing back to his friends in Memphis, saying 'I'm not with you guys anymore.' There was also a lot of conflict between Greg and Max in the studio, so maybe Greg also thought it was Max's way of winning that argument in the end. Everyone's so sensitive—such a sensitive group of men!"

Adding to the friction were Cartwright's attempts to take a producer's position in the record, which, McCabe-Lokos recalls, he did not tell the group he'd been paid by the label to do. (Ethier shrugs this off, saying that Cartwright received no more than a couple of hundred dollars extra for the position.) Consequently, says McCabe-Lokos, Cartwright exerted unexplained influence over the session, which the band envisioned being produced by all of them.

The conflict seemed insurmountable, and part way through the recording process, McCabe-Lokos pulled the original Snakes aside and told them he was quitting the band.

Ethier remembers, "Max said, 'I'll finish this record, but I'm not going to continue in this band.' Because it wasn't his band anymore. A part of it was that he was sulking because he couldn't yell at everyone in front of a stranger. But another thing was that it just wasn't our band. It was too unfocused because of Greg. So he quit—and then Andrew talked him out of it. He was saying, 'There are so many things that we want to do as a band that we haven't done yet. Please don't quit.' And within that conversation, Max backed down."

Despite being held uneasily together, the Deadly Snakes set out to tour behind *I'm Not Your Soldier Anymore*, drafting an interim bassist named Randy to fill in during the tour. From the beginning, Randy was a poor match for the band.

"Randy's a really, really nice guy," says Moszynski. "It just wasn't fitting. I don't think he had much travel experience in a band situation, so he was breaking all these basic rules, like—don't just wander off, and don't threaten to call your mom for money to fly home. He said those exact words, 'I can just call my mom and have her send me money, and I'll fly home.' And Jer [Madsen] just turns to me and goes, 'Holy shit.' There are dos and do-not-dos, and he was checking off that second list really quickly. At that point we had all toured so many times for the previous two or three years, we had become a fairly disciplined, functioning group. We managed to keep shit together—don't get lost, don't just vanish. You sacrifice a lot of travel liberties if you're doing it in a band. You can't just go on tangents: you're travelling as a unit."

Randy also insisted, whenever the band had downtime, on bringing CDs of his solo project Randwiches to consign at local record stores across the U.S.

"I remember being so mad," Moszynski says. "He would sell these CDs on the basis of being 'in the Deadly Snakes.' Everyone was so livid—it was such a ridiculous looking album that he had. We were like, 'We do not want this associated with us in any way. This is your first, and looking like it'll be your last, tour.'"

In terms of live performance, though, the Snakes were at the top of their game. Several members recall the apex of their tour occurring at New York City's landmark bar Manitoba's (owned by Handsome Dick Manitoba, frontman of formative mid-70s punk band the Dictators) in late summer of 2001.

"Oh my god, that was the best! It was such a fantastic night," Moszynski remembers. "We're all at Manitoba's and it's starting to get late. We were supposed to play at midnight and it's 11:30—so we're going, 'Where's Greg? We play in half an hour, but we need him to be here so we can start.' He had run off with his friend Dan Rose, who's a fully ordained Voodoo priest. I stayed with him one time—he gave me his spare bedroom; I lay down on the bed, and he came in and lit these small fires around the bed to purify the room or something? Which was interesting. He was also hanging out with his friend Bill [Pietsch], from the Church Keys, who has since died. [Pietsch] made that Manitoba's show so fantastic by yelling nonsense non-stop. Between songs you'd hear this distinctive voice shoot out among the crowd: 'My mouth... is prettier than your face!' and 'You gotta go to the well... to get the water!' Somehow he got a tambourine and he kept framing his face with it.

"So it's 11:30, and we're trying to find Greg. Someone said he was down at the Lakeside Lounge, a five-minute walk away. Matt went over to the Lakeside to grab him, saying, 'Greg! We gotta go!' They're all blind, blasted drunk. Greg looks up, sees it's Matt, goes, 'Okay!' Looks down, throws up into double-cupped hands, and then is escorted back to Manitoba's, where we put on one of our best shows—one of those shows that was total chaos from start to finish. I don't think Manitoba's is [even] set up for a three-piece band. We had Matt and Jer behind the bar—there were seven guys in the Snakes at that point. It was crazy. But it turns out you can pull of a really good show even after puking into your hands."

In footage now available on YouTube, the band blazes sweat-slick through "I've Gotta Plan (For Saturday Night)" like they're wracked with convulsions. Ethier wails into the mic for the verse; McCabe-Lokos—shirtless and frenzied, pounding a tambourine in the parts of the song that don't call for organ—and Cartwright shout the response at each other across Ethier's microphone. After the instruments drop out, McCabe-Lokos grabs the mic to holler the lead into the last chorus. It's absolutely electrifying, practically the Platonic form of a perfect rock and roll show: wild, sweaty, ecstatic and loud.

On the second-last date of the Canada-U.S. tour for *I'm Not Your Soldier Anymore*, Ethier, Madsen and Cartwright ate lunch together in Austin, Texas. They discussed the ongoing problems they'd been having with Randy, whose fate in the band was by that point already sealed. Ethier remembers, Cartwright said, "I don't know if I should still play in the band, but if we continue, Randy has to go. I can't tour with that guy." Cartwright offered to find a replacement bassist; Madsen and Ethier agreed they'd look into it after they got home.

"Then, at the end of that tour," says Ethier, "Greg was no longer in the band."

"It was easy," says McCabe-Lokos. "He lived in Memphis."

Ethier regrets not being clearer with Cartwright about the end of his part in the Deadly Snakes. He feels some guilt about resorting to passive dismissal, but recognizes that Cartwright was a poor fit for the band.

"I fully supported the idea of not keeping Greg in the band," he says. "We couldn't write all together and be a band with this guy from outside."

"There are some moments that I'm not proud of on some of those tours with him," McCabe-Lokos says. "But we functioned on our own level, with our roles, until he got added to it. Then it just didn't work. And there were egos involved—we did not want him to steal the show."

Ethier goes on: "I think Greg didn't realize how big a deal that band was to us. He'd been through a lot of bands, and to him, it was just another band he was going to play in before he got his other band, Reigning Sound, off the ground. But he was stepping into a really dense jungle of people who'd known each other a really long time, and have intense friendships and relationships. I don't think he was expecting how defined the band was already, and how difficult it would be to find a place in something that already had all its places filled."

Cartwright could sense their impending separation long before it occurred. "None of it hurts my feelings," he says. "I realized when we were making [*I'm Not Your Soldier*] that I wasn't going to be able to play with them anymore. I didn't want to disrupt the natural balance that was already there and I figured that it'd be a healthier band without an interloper. And their best work came after that record."

———

The Deadly Snakes ended their musical relationship with

Greg Cartwright at the end of the summer of 2001. They had completed their U.S. tour with him (and Randy) on a Sunday night in Austin, Texas, and, immediately following their last show, drove the 1,000 kilometres overnight back to Cartwright's house in Memphis.

At the end of the 10-hour drive, they staggered out of the van onto the cool of Cartwright's lawn. It was a sunny afternoon, and Cartwright had arranged a show of garage-rock luminaries that night featuring the White Stripes—whose soon-to-be-breakthrough third album *White Blood Cells* had just been released. Most of the Snakes were looking forward to it.

"It's supposed to be the end-of-tour party," says Moszynski, "where we can wrap it up, hang out, drink for free and just get to be dudes for one more night. We were going to spend the day lazing around Greg's house as a reward for the tour being done."

Some of the band members were trying to sleep when McCabe-Lokos announced that he felt it imperative that the band return home as soon as possible, and insisted (with support from Jeremi Madsen) that the Snakes pile back into the van and press on immediately.

"We were the only two drivers," Madsen recalls, "and for whatever reason, we wanted to get home."

As on all their tours, whoever was driving got to decide the travel schedule, so, despite the lure of the evening's entertainment, they bid their final goodbye to Cartwright, climbed back in the van, and set out on an appalling 15-hour, 1,500-kilometre drive. Having already driven through the previous night, the band was running entirely on ephedrine pills purchased at truck stops along the way.

"We were popping that trucker speed like Tic Tacs," Moszynski says. "They were just so available. Every truck stop. This miracle pill is supposed to wake us up with 'no side effects'—meanwhile it makes you completely insane. I'm popping those like nobody's business, while the drive just keeps going and going." Most memorably, Moszynski recalls seeing a 40-foot Elvis Presley dancing on the roof of a car dealership.

"I suspect now that it was probably one of those wavy-arm blow-up things," he says, "but to my eyes, I thought, 'Oh, fuck: It's the King!' I was twisted out of my skull."

Dawn had broken on their second straight night of driving as they crossed the border into Canada. After refusing to listen to Randy's Randwiches CD for the entire tour, the band finally relented and let him put it on: everyone I discussed it with recalls finding it excruciating.

They cleared customs at 7:45 a.m.; it was the morning of September 11th, 2001. Stuck in morning gridlock on the 401 from Windsor, ephedrine-scrambled after over 24-hours of driving, and unable to listen to any more of Randwiches, they turned the radio on.

Says Madsen, "It took us a second before we started cluing in, you know? Saying, 'Wait, did they just say "it fell"? What fell? The twin towers? Aren't they in New York?'"

"I was convinced it was some *War Of The Worlds* bullshit," Moszynski remembers, "until we realized every station was talking about it. Even Howard Stern. Obviously something was really fucked up. Meanwhile I'm hallucinating in the van. My mind was just so fucked already, and then getting this news…"

He shakes his head with a look of disbelief, and continues, "When I got dropped off—I was living in my parents' place at the time—and I bolted out of the van, ran into the house and told my mom, 'It's the end of the world!' And my mom ran into my sister on her way out the door and she said, 'Don't talk to Andrew. I think he's on acid.' I turned on the TV and parked myself in front of it, and thought, 'I'm not moving. I'm going to be watching this for the next 12 fucking hours. I'm going to watch this whole thing unfold.' Then in two minutes I was asleep."

"We were so lucky we made that drive when we did," says Madsen. Almost immediately after the Snakes crossed the border, it was sealed off behind them.

Multi-instrumentalist Matt Carlson adds, "If we hadn't driven back that day, we'd have been stuck there forever."

CHAPTER 6

TROUBLE'S GONNA STAY A WHILE

"If the band was a body, Max was the heart, the one pumping the blood, keeping it going. But Matt was the soul. Matt was everything good about that band." – André Ethier

THE DEADLY SNAKES emerged a different band following the race to the border and their separation from Greg Cartwright. Tiring of the simplistic expression garage rock demanded of them, the maturing Snakes wanted to consider and convey more complex feelings and ideas.

"We were all getting over the debt that we had to previous bands and the genre we'd chosen to play in," Ethier explains. "It's something that happens in a younger person's mind. You say, 'I'm from Toronto—I'm not Greg Cartwright, I'm not from Memphis, or Detroit, or even the States. My experience is different, so I have to hide that to be like them.' We were fans of that music, but saw ourselves as subservient to it *because* we were fans."

Thus the image of the Snakes' flight from Memphis—from Cartwright, and even from the company of the White

Stripes—seems symbolic for a band cutting themselves free of their influences and defining themselves on their own terms. Escaping home to Toronto, they left behind all that had gotten them where they were.

"They wanted me to help them," says Cartwright. "And they wanted that connection with my name. But it's a weird dynamic, because there comes a time when you feel you want to succeed on your own."

Ethier explains, "Once we saw the weaknesses of Greg as a person—not his weaknesses, but just the fact that he wanted to play with *us*!—that validated our personalities and let us feel ourselves starting to shine. You can see it happening on *I'm Not Your Soldier Anymore*, awkwardly, then more confidently on the next record. I don't want to put down Greg at all, but once we removed Greg from the band, we had, in a sense, eaten our influences—we'd consumed them and rejected them, and from that point on we went on confidently doing whatever we wanted to do."

The Snakes recruited placid, long-haired bassist Chad Ross, then 25, who had known Ethier and McCabe-Lokos since high school.

"I was so excited," Ross remembers. "I truly loved their music; I loved the band. At the time it wasn't like the original line-up of the Snakes: there was a bit more maturity after those five years."

Ross—described teasingly by several as a "pot-smoking hippie"—has kind eyes and an air of serene patience that rivals Ethier's placidity. He returns continually to grateful praise for the band, both as musicians and as friends.

"My fondest memories," Ross tells me, "are of discovering

the camaraderie behind this tight-knit group of friends. It was pretty rowdy, and it continued to be rowdy right up to the end. There were bad times, but there were way more good, funny times. I have the utmost respect for all those guys. Each of them is an artist."

"Thank God we found Chad," says Ethier. "There was an initial burst of energy at the beginning, but then there was a couple of years of disarray, with Greg half in and half not in. Once Chad joined, instantly, we knew that was the band, no more changes."

"Chad joining meant we had another *musician* in the band, rather than just a bass player," says McCabe-Lokos. "His musicianship made us all work a little harder. And because he was a new guy, there was no question of him overstepping his boundaries."

Outside of the reactive relationship between Ethier and McCabe-Lokos, the rest of the Snakes were uniquely even-tempered, and Ross, with his innate tranquility, fit well among them.

When the three of us meet over pizza, Ross and Moszynski, now playing together in riff-rock powerhouse Quest For Fire (along with *Porcella* engineer Josh Bauman), talk with the timing and humour that comes from spending years together in vans. Ross is quieter, listening a long time before speaking up, while Moszynski, with his easy grin, talks candidly, his voice deep and wry. He's the most laid back of an already chill group, and his personality is an extension of his sense of humour. Having always been the youngest member of the band, Moszynski maintains an unflappable joviality about the Snakes, their membership, and their history that implies he was able to derive more fun from their decade together than those ensnarled in personal politics. He grins constantly and laughs often; life as he lives it seems like a pretty good time. Affable and talkative, Moszynski gets stopped everywhere we go in Toronto by friends who want to spend a few minutes catching up.

The Snakes' horn section, saxophonist Jeremi Madsen and trumpet player Matt Carlson, are taciturn by contrast. There's nothing unpleasant about their initial silence, but when I call Madsen, he politely defers to the rest of the band, maintaining that because he didn't participate in the songwriting he doesn't have much to say, and claiming that everyone else can speak more eloquently than he can. Carlson, known as the shyest member of the Snakes but also their creative engine, doesn't even return my call—as Moszynski had warned me might happen.

Carlson works by day in construction, alongside Ross, and recently totally remodelled André and Kai Ethier's kitchen (the results were photographed for *Canadian House and Home* magazine where Kai Ethier works). Madsen, until recently, worked with Carlson and Ross, but decided to return to school for forestry; he's since gotten married (all the Snakes attended the wedding) and moved to the country outside Toronto. Today, he works for Ontario Parks. ("He's a hearty Canadian lad," says Ethier.)

At Moszynski's insistence, the retiring Madsen and Carlson accompany him to meet me for an evening at the Rhino, and both slowly and good-naturedly join in the conversation. I later learn that Moszynski didn't tell Carlson they'd be meeting me until they'd already left his house. Madsen, a husky good-time hoser with a rural Ontario burr in his voice, delights in telling stories of the band's most extreme moments. He and Carlson energetically disagree, for example, over whether their preposterous non-stop drive from Vancouver to Toronto at the end of one Canadian tour took 52 or 56 straight hours, while agreeing on memories of excess liquor and drug consumption. But Madsen goes quiet at more serious questions about the band's legacy.

"I'm pretty content with what I did," Madsen says with a comfortable shrug. "I'm happy now just to settle down and stay home. I haven't picked up the sax since the last show. I'm amazed I still own it, to be honest."

"I don't think he had picked it up prior to the first time we played, either, except playing in high school," Ethier says later.

Carlson—boyish and affable, his ball cap pulled low over shy eyes—says even less, but will quietly add a sentence or a joke here and there. Simultaneously the most reserved and the most vital member of the band, he's enigmatic. His mastery of a wide variety of instruments, coupled with his ease at writing songs and perfecting other Snakes' numbers, is crucial to the widening sound of the band's later years. Each individual Snake goes out of his way to sing the praises of Carlson's innate musical genius.

"You can't even put a number on it in terms of song-writing credits, because he has such an incredible instinct for picking up on the little things that are missing and need to be filled in," Moszynski says. "He plays everything—trumpet, guitar, harmonica, bass on a bunch of stuff; you can stick him anywhere and he'll come up with something perfect. You'd never be able to get him to take credit for how much he put into something, though. I'd be saying, 'Matt, you saved this song. You came up with *the* hook,' but he'd never acknowledge how crucial his parts or his songs were."

"If the band was a body," Ethier says, "Max was the heart, the one pumping the blood, keeping it going. But Matt was the soul. Matt was everything good about that band."

I ask Ethier if there would be any way I could get Carlson to speak on the record in more detail. Ethier responds, "He's really shy and I don't think he likes to be put on the spot. He's loyal to his friends and wouldn't want to see anything that he said in print hurt anybody. When he has the choice, I would assume he'd just as soon not choose to put himself in that position. He just understands the bigger picture. He's thoughtful enough to know the difference between private conversation and public conversation."

Carlson's bashfulness worked against him in the band's creative process, however. Ethier noticed that Carlson was growing resigned as the band went on, "because the others would appropriate his songs and rewrite them, often dumbing them down, knowing he was too quiet to fight over it. And he'd let us, but he became really sad, and I remember him saying he was going to stop writing songs for the Snakes because he had these ideas that were supposed to work a certain way, but because Max and I were so busy with our own concerns, we'd just take his songs and say, 'This is how it works easiest for us right now,' meaning we never nurtured or developed those songs."

"If the band was a person," Ethier continues, "[Carlson would] be the kindness of that person. It was overshadowed a lot by what overshadows goodness in real people—ego, deceit, self-centredness, my own self-centredness or competition with another person in the band, because Max and I have bigger personalities. But I wonder if at some point the Snakes could have evolved and gotten better because we allowed Matt to come further into the light. He and Andrew and Chad and Jer—those guys often seem like supporting players to Max and me because we sing, but they were the ones who made the whole thing a lot better."

I ask Moszynski if he feels that he and Carlson didn't get enough credit for their contribution to the Snakes' repertoire, and he responds with a characteristic chuckle.

"I know I wrote those songs!" he says. "People I know around Toronto seem to view the Snakes as a whole, not as just a singer-songwriter project. I'm not going to lose any sleep over it."

It seems that Carlson, out of all the Snakes, lost the most when the group disbanded. Ethier, in addition to his art career, still records albums and tours. McCabe-Lokos has thrown his creative energy into acting but in recent years has occasionally played music with ex-Snakes, joining Carlson and Moszynski in backing Ethier on a 7-inch single released by Texas record label Dull Knife in 2009. McCabe-Lokos also started a short-lived art rock band called the Rats of Spring with Moszynski, Ethier, Dallas Good of the Sadies, and a number of the musicians who've backed Ethier on his solo releases[5].

Ross and Moszynski play and tour together with Quest for Fire; as well, Ross records with Nordic Nomadic, his

---

5 For their sole show, they played two 10-minute Velvet Underground covers (one of which was "Sister Ray," which they light-heartedly cut down from 17 minutes) amid a cacophony of four guitars.

solo project, and Moszynski plays with Toronto band Cattle, as well as with Ethier in a new project called Cut Flowers. Madsen no longer plays much, but has been the organizer of a musicians' hockey league in Toronto. While the others pursue their own creative drives, Carlson, however, still has the desire to play, but no longer has the musical edifice of the Snakes or other bands to support that need.

"I like playing," he says, "and I want to play more. But I don't really want to tour. I miss recording and playing songs. I play at home and record things—little riffs and stuff like that."

Carlson, Ethier and Moszynski have begun to try out Carlson's new songs with him in his apartment.

"He has a bunch of songs he's written—he's always writing," Ethier says, "and he wants to play. but I don't think he has any interest at all in playing live. He just wants to record and do it for personal reasons—for fun. It's always fun."

When I ask Carlson if he got what he wanted out of the band, he says simply, "I was never doing it for money or recognition or glory."

After a second of expectant silence, Madsen, with disarming tenderness, prompts him for more, asking "Did you get something, though? Did you have fun?"

Carlson smiles, beneath the brim of his ball cap, and nods gently.

"Of course," he says, and he leaves it at that.

———

Though the Deadly Snakes had coalesced in membership and vision, they hadn't outgrown their defining tensions. Most famously, the band came within belligerent inches of splitting up at the end of a 2002 spring tour. As they finished their set at New York's Mercury Lounge, McCabe-Lokos insulted Ethier into the microphone and Ethier took a run at him.

"We're in fucking New York City," Ethier remembers, "and the crowd wanted an encore. They were cheering. I didn't know Max was mad, so I said, 'Hey Max, they want an encore. Let's do it.' And he said, 'Fuck you, man. You fucked up that song. I'm not playing an encore.' I was shocked. For a second I was speechless—then I chased him off the stage, into the audience."

Carlson, fuming, manhandled McCabe-Lokos out of the audience and away from Ethier, dragging him into the back until Ethier's rage subsided.

Ethier shakes his head. "*Everyone* was mad at Max at that point," he says, "because that's shitty. So I made a mistake? Just play another fucking song. I should have punched him out."

"I was doing the merch table," laughs Moszynski, "and I sold a tonne of T-shirts and stuff by telling people that it was probably the last Deadly Snakes show. I don't remember where we stayed that night, but I remember the drive to Montreal the next day was the most silent we'd ever been. Generally, between the six of us there would be conversations all day long, talking bullshit until we get to the next city. But that drive to Montreal was so tense, and so quiet. You didn't want to be the guy to try to start a conversation and be shot down."

McCabe-Lokos admits, "At the time, I was always like, 'We gotta be more professional! We have to play without fucking up!' And I'd fuck up too—everybody fucks up. But at the time, I thought André was making a lot of mistakes. In my head, he wasn't trying to do it properly and he thought it was okay to play bad. So we fought. I fought with guys in the band. One time we had a bit of a fistfight—it was fucking me versus all of them, too! I was such an asshole."

"If he remembers it as him trying to fight some of us," Ethier says dryly, "it didn't really work that way. It's more that he was attacked by us. By three of us."

Ethier demurs when I ask him to elaborate. When I persist, he says, "There was a moment where—no punches were thrown—but Max was just behaving really badly towards three people who were in their underwear trying to go to sleep in a hotel room. They were being shouted at—berated. Then he got thrown across the hotel room and held down to be told to shut up. If he sees it as him trying to fight us all, that's just the most ridiculous thing."

Yet in spite of the friction in the band, Ross remembers the Snakes as being increasingly bound together by camaraderie. What kept the band from dissolution, he says, was "male energy, enthusiasm, all these wonderful things about youth. You can hear it when you listen to those records."

McCabe-Lokos agrees that male friendship was central to the Snakes. "When you've got only guys around you, you can say what you want, and it's gross, it's vulgar. There's a certain understanding among male friends, a humour that exists that everybody gets, and if there was a woman, that'd be different. It was such a cliché, particularly in how it looked to a guy's girlfriend if she came to a show on tour or something. Because I guess it was a boy's club. It doesn't seem mean-spirited—but we were brethren."

He goes on, "There was very, very briefly a girl playing

trumpet in the band at the beginning, but that didn't last very long. We were playing a show and she dyed her hair bright pink. She came to practice and—I don't know what I was thinking, but I said, 'What the fuck did you do? You look like an idiot! No!' And she cried. It was mean. But I was thinking, 'You're in *our* band and you're making us look like some kind of ska outfit!'"

"It would have been very difficult had there been a female presence throughout," says Moszynski. Especially for young men, he reflects, a band can be like a bathroom, in which the dirty particulars of manhood can be revealed without the threat of embarrassment before the opposite gender. "Being in a band entails sitting in a van staring forward, or sitting in a hotel room staring at the TV, with the same four or five guys non-stop for years on end," he says. "Inevitably you'll end up talking about every possible thing you know. With a girl around, that leaves out several key areas that you can comfortably bring up."

The male bonding in the band frequently went from discussion to action. Various members of the Snakes ruefully relate stories from their early days that, true to form, involve vomit, defecation, masturbation and every manner of misbehaviour undergone in the comfort of all-male company.

"When you're young," Ethier says of friendships among men, "it starts out as a gang mentality that protects everyone. Hopefully it develops into camaraderie—but even that needs to be set aside. Male camaraderie can be very dangerous, especially as you get older; it's a type of arrested development that keeps you from fully realizing your potential. I believe in the individual, and that's crucial."

CHAPTER 7
ODE TO JOY

"I wanted a room full of people to sing along in abandon, like, *Fuck it! We're all gonna die!*" – Max McCabe-Lokos

A YEAR AFTER CUTTING their ties with Cartwright and racing to the border on the early morning of September 11th, the Deadly Snakes recorded their third album, *Ode to Joy*. They released it in April 2003, and by all accounts, it was the finest thing the band had ever done. Every Snake calls it the best of their four records, and a wide variety of reviewers—no longer just punk/garage rock purists—hailed it as a masterpiece. Notoriously snotty tastemakers Pitchfork rated the record 8.5 on 10, calling it "an explosive, knee-bending kick in the pants."

A loud, raw, minimalist record, *Ode to Joy* offered an entirely new sound nonetheless consistent with the Snakes' trajectory. It is, finally, the band growing up and leaving home, facing the world on their own. Reaching beyond the landscape of American garage rock that they'd escaped, it refers all the way back to the gospel roots of the soul and R&B the Snakes grew up on, but merges that sound with a strong nod to their Toronto forbears the Band, the prototypical group of Canadians self-consciously playing American music.

The album opens *in medias res*, like a door into a room where the Snakes are playing at top volume, the whole band roaring together from the first beat, the first *second*, with Ethier in *Subterranean Homesick*–form howling the lyrics to "Closed Casket" commandingly over the din.

From the first, *Ode to Joy* sounds different than any previous Snakes release. Its most conspicuous characteristic is its sparseness—following the sonic indulgence of *Not Your Soldier*, on which some songs have guitar on as many as three tracks, the band agreed in advance that no song on *Ode to Joy* would have more than one guitar.

As a result, *Ode to Joy* allows other instruments to rise to prominence, most notably McCabe-Lokos's gurgling organ and Chad Ross's virtuosic bass. But also, there are spaces, quiet parts, and single instruments speaking for the group, all a measure of a band's confidence in the talent inherent in their collectively pooled songwriting. And when (in the masterful dark pop number "Sink Like Stones"[6]) the song drops down to just the organ tracing Ross's melancholic bass-line before gradually reintroducing each instrument from quiet, you can feel how convinced the Deadly Snakes are that what they're doing is right.

Ethier's songs—poised and Dylan-influenced—are more accomplished than ever, but the surprise of the album is the emerging voice of McCabe-Lokos, who sings lead on five of

---

6 Ethier notes that part of the song's lyrical inspiration came from a bet between him and McCabe-Lokos to see which of the two could fit the most references to animals into a song.

12 songs. His frenzied delivery is in distinct contrast with Ethier's stentorian self-assurance, and presents him as a dramatic character, by turns passionate, ecstatic, hysterical, melancholic and derisive.

There are other notable differences between *Ode to Joy* and any previous Snakes release—in spite of its willingness to be quiet, it's actually *louder*, the production at times creeping so frantically into the red that it rings like the buzz of tinnitus. And though the Snakes were always a wild band, the energy of the record is manic instead of rollicking, edgy instead of ballsy. Where before they had the cockiness of insecure kids trying to convince the world of their worth, they now played with the blithe confidence of grown men well trained in their craft.

"We had achieved something very naturally with *Ode to Joy*," says Ethier. "The energy of knowing that we were finally a band, that's what finally produced it. We were at our peak then, and without a lot of effort we created a cohesive record that feels good all the way through."

Ode to Joy's disavowal of garage rock convention was a key moment in the band's development. The Snakes that began life knee-deep in burger wrappers had gone from the red meat rock and roll of garage tradition to a multi-course musical meal of their own design. *Ode to Joy* shows a band grown up enough that they've finally moved out of their parents' house—be that the genre from which they emerged, the influence of their heroes, the insecurity of their membership, or, most likely, a blend of all those things.

The record was a landmark release in Canadian rock and roll. At the same time as Toronto-based indie successes Broken Social Scene, Stars, Metric and their related side-projects were riding high around the world on widely acclaimed pop albums that were commendable and catchy but totally safe, *Ode to Joy* presented the Snakes bridling with aggression and agitation, but also with rumination, depth and the titular joy. The album had the range of pop but retained the spiteful volatility of the Snakes' insular gang years, which made it decidedly different from the cheery but languid bands that then as now, define Toronto's music for the world.

"I hate how fucking chummy Canadian indie rock is," complains Snakes' mentor Chris Trowbridge. "It feels like such bullshit, like everyone's trying to pad their resumes. I know it's a small scene and you can be supportive and all that, but there's something to be said for being fucking singular. For being one thing: a rock and roll band, and being true to yourselves, not part of a rock-and-roll-by-committee establishment, which is what it's settled into. I don't have anything personal against those guys, but Broken Social Scene and all that shit, to me, it's like fucking summer camp.

"Why does it have to be like that? I'd rather hear six guys or women or whoever, who have an aesthetic that's refined and tested against one another and try to create something. It doesn't have to be 100% original—it just has to be good at what it is. Now everything has to be everything to everybody, and it's not rock and roll anymore."

The innovation of *Ode to Joy* comes largely as a result of the charged creativity between André Ethier and the emerging voice of Max McCabe-Lokos. Each of Ethier's songs flashes with energy and inspiration, from the minimalist tent-revival stomp of "Oh My Bride" to the Dylan-influenced rock of "Everybody Seems to Think (You've Got Some Kind of

Hold on Me)" to his last song on the album, the exceptional "Sink Like Stones," which is surely one of the band's finest recorded moments. But McCabe-Lokos's sudden appearance as a lead singer has an equally powerful effect.

"I had become more confident as a musician," says McCabe-Lokos, "and I thought, 'I can sing more songs, so I'm going to.' I hadn't really written much before then—it took a couple of years for me to get the chops down to do something like that."

"I was kind of surprised," says Ethier of McCabe-Lokos's emergence as a co-vocalist. I had passively assumed that I was the main singer in the band, and I could feel him moving toward that position. I was arguing with him more then."

On *Not Your Soldier*, McCabe-Lokos's lead on "Pirate Cowboy" sounds like an anomaly—it's a fun, quirky song that you could take as a novelty number. His introduction on *Ode to Joy* as a lead singer is all the more startling because his songs are suddenly so dark. "I Can't Sleep at Night," the album's second track, is restless with his hectic ranting; "Burn Down the Valley" is a frenzy of apocalyptic images; and album closer "Mutiny & Lonesome Blues" is a vitriolic burst of organ-stomping hysteria.

It's "I Want to Die," however—a contender for the album's finest song—that refines McCabe-Lokos's vocal persona and builds the structure of character that will carry him through to the band's end. Over the bright throb of the Snakes' take on a gospel rave-up[7], McCabe-Lokos testifies agitatedly to the end of optimism, the loss of faith and the

---

[7] McCabe-Lokos says the interplay in "I Want to Die" between the nimble, high guitar and the workhorse bass-line was an idea he borrowed from a favourite Staples Singers number.

futility of caring.

"I wasn't suicidal," he says, "but I wanted to match dark or melancholy lyrics with really cheery, Christmassy sort of music. I wanted a room full of people to sing along in abandon, like, *Fuck it! We're all gonna die!*"

When, in the same song, McCabe-Lokos sings, "I haven't always done the best I can/but I learned to be alone/and I learned to be a man," it's a statement that could represent the sum of his, and the band's, expression on *Ode to Joy*. The album considers everything that got it where it is, for better or worse, and it knows where it came from, but it also understands the new and different creature it is now. This is the music of people who have finally grown up—a little. They're still capable of the bloody-knuckle piano and band-saw guitar that's all over the record, but at other times they play with an astonishing reflection that would have been unthinkable on the previous two records.

Ode to Joy's signature sound was no accident: McCabe-Lokos purposefully set out from the beginning to produce the record.

"I figured Greg was a mistake," he says. "I didn't want to let something like that happen again, so I grabbed the thing by the horns. There was too much of people saying, you know, 'I don't know who does that... it just gets done.' I thought, fuck that. There's gonna be no mistake about if somebody's producing it or not."

McCabe-Lokos's production gives the record a startling sound that's both brittle and heavy, rudely underlining the instability of its governing emotions. When I heard it for the first time, I didn't get it—the record had little of the lo-fi quality of the previous two albums. The polish on it cast a sickly gleam. The aesthetic of the album makes internal sense, but on the first couple of listens, its shimmery thickness feels like the visionary product of a head injury.

Andrew Moszynski remembers a critical tension during the recording of *Ode to Joy*.

"André's such a naturally gifted guy," he says. "He had all these songs to choose from, and Max immediately vetoed half of them and forced a bunch of his own songs onto the record. He was even writing the songs in the studio—the sort of situation where he needed to finish the lyrics to a song because he had to go sing it in five minutes."

While McCabe-Lokos's lyrics have weak points (notably in "I'm Leaving You": "Explanations for what I might do/ is just another reason I love you") the emergence of his exaggerated and volatile voice is instrumental to the success of the record. His voice, above all, lends a spirit of ambition and independence that—together with Ethier's confidence and experimentation—marks the album as the expression of an older, wiser band. For all the musical success of *Ode to Joy*, however, McCabe-Lokos's drive for co-frontman status had to come at the expense of the band's existing voice.

Ethier says, "At that point I began to see the future of the Snakes as either I could step up my will in the band and exert myself more, fight with Max for control so that I'd be happier and feel properly represented, or I could take a passive route where I tried to work better within the group and facilitate records being made by being more open to what other people wanted, but make my own records on the side where I didn't have any conflict and I could do what I wanted."

CHAPTER 8
MUTINY AND LONESOME BLUES

"It's a lesson for anyone—if you try to dominate a situation, eventually you may win and dominate a group, but by that point you'll have lost a lot of the inspiration or the creative energy that you had originally wanted to get out of these people." – André Ethier

IF *Ode to Joy* WAS the Deadly Snakes' finest achievement, it also scored the fissures of the band's eventual disintegration. Following the completion and release of the album, Ethier combined his surfeit of unrecorded songs with his long-standing intention to record a solo album backed by several other Snakes along with an old friend, pianist Christopher Sandes. Ethier didn't tell McCabe-Lokos about the plan, let alone that the other musicians on the album would be Moszynski and Carlson, making it a cast of three quarters of the original Snakes with a new piano player in McCabe-Lokos's place. They began recording while McCabe-Lokos was in Portugal on a five-month movie shoot.

"I got back into town," says McCabe-Lokos, "and everyone was acting really weird. I'd call Matt to go get a beer, and he'd be all shifty and say, 'I, uh, can't. I… uh, gotta go to the uh… studio.' 'Why?' 'Uh… no reason, really…' It made me really angry because they were tiptoeing around me."

"The way I saw it," Ethier explains slowly, "was that they were musicians that I knew and wanted to play with. They weren't writing songs, they were just playing drums and bass to facilitate this record that I did with my friend Christopher. I remember thinking maybe I should get musicians other than the guys that were in the Snakes, but then I started thinking the only reason I'm doing that is for Max. And that annoyed me, that he couldn't just be okay with it and I had to do that for his feelings. Ultimately he was okay. But we did change their names—they went on the record uncredited [they would be billed as "Pickles and Price"], and that was *for Max*. We weren't trying to take the Snakes away from him."

"I don't care that André made a solo record," McCabe-Lokos says with an air of uncertain indifference, "but it was with Matt and Andrew and… fuck! I still think it's weird that of all the musicians in the city, he chose those ones. He was even so careful about it that he didn't credit them. He maybe just thought it was what it was, that it was distasteful to make a solo record with members of the band that you're in. It was so underhanded and seedy. It was dishonest."

Reflecting on the friction that arose from McCabe-Lokos's rise to vocalist in the band, Ethier explains, "In a sense, though the record was for me because I wanted to do it, and it was also for Chris, my friend who I'd always planned on making a record with, I also saw it as a way of facilitating the Snakes as a process. I didn't try to get In the Red to put it out. I didn't want to upstage the Snakes—I got it put out on a small label, and I hardly did any shows. It wasn't a new career. But Max is pretty sensitive about these things, and I knew it would hurt his feelings. I remember it being really hard to tell him, and I was avoiding telling him. But that goes to show the kind of personality he has—anyone doing something without him can be perceived as a slight against him. He really wanted everyone to be his employees, almost, in his band. That's harsh, but he had power issues where anyone doing anything undermined his authority. He didn't want other people to see it as though we had to do it because he was an asshole—which wasn't the truth anyway, but you know. Ultimately it didn't affect him at all."

"The irresponsibility of organizing something like that sort of coup, it was so insulting," says McCabe-Lokos. "And I probably decided then that the Deadly Snakes was my band—I figured, like, 'Okay then, your band is this thing of André with these guys, and if you want to do that, then the other thing IS my band, and I'm in charge of it.'"

"By the end," Ethier remembers, "[McCabe-Lokos] slowly came to dominate the band, and people slowly gave up control to him, but by the time he dominated the band it was a band that was no longer passionate. That was the irony. It's a lesson for anyone—if you try to dominate a situation, eventually you may win and dominate a group, but by that point you'll have lost a lot of the inspiration or the creative energy that you had originally wanted to get out of these people."

By the end of the out-of-town dates for *Ode to Joy*, the Snakes concluded that they didn't want to tour anymore, either.

"All through that post-*Ode to Joy* era," Ethier says, "I was always thinking that I'd quit the band, or that the band should break up, even though I wasn't going to be the one to do it. I remember having a conversation with Max and him saying, 'Let's stop touring. It's not fun anymore. It's a young man's job, unless you're successful.' So we both agreed we'd stop touring, which seemed like the perfect solution."

The next day, however, the Snakes received a call from Swedish garage-rock sensations the Hives inviting them out on tour, and they decided it was worth signing on for. The tour took them to major venues, but it changed little about the band when it ended. When they were once more on the road by themselves, the Snakes faced poor promotion and small crowds in cities they should have been able to sell out.

"If you're travelling in a band of eight people that nobody knows and nobody's going to give you more than $200 a show, it's totally idiotic," says Greg Cartwright. "You're doomed."

"We were still slugging away, but it wasn't picking up," says Chad Ross.

Moszynski says flatly, "The tours just got worse and worse."

"It's fun when you're young," Ethier says, "because it's an adventure, but as you get older it's just a money-losing situation that you repeat over and over again."

"Our relationship with touring," says McCabe-Lokos, "was based on bad promotion. We'd get to the club, we wouldn't be listed in the newspaper and there'd be no posters. Promotion is so integral, and too often there was just none of it. For example, we played Seattle before, and the first couple of shows were great, but then the last time, we showed up and there's no one there… it didn't make sense to me."

The Snakes themselves, however, were not given to promoting themselves, and had never been interested in participating in the kind of industry mechanisms that might lead to fame.

"At one point we interviewed someone as a manager," Ethier remembers, "and everything they said they would do for us was totally in opposition to what we wanted to do. They wanted us to go out on a lot of tours, do magazine shoots, but we didn't want to do any of that. At that point, really early on, it became our lowest priority to try and make it as a band, to do it as a career. We just wanted to make records and do small tours when we wanted to. When you want to be bigger, it's morally compromising. You find yourself saying, 'There's this show that's going to suck, but it's in front of a lot of people and we have to do it because the record company wants us to.' So we avoided all that, and it was good for us."

"The idea formed early on that we're not the band who puts on makeup and doesn't wear their own clothes for photo shoots," McCabe-Lokos explains, nodding to the late-90s trend of garage bands posing in swinging London garb, eyeshadow and teased hair.

The band tried signing a licensing deal with Toronto's Paper Bag records, home of Broken Social Scene and Stars, allowing Paper Bag to distribute their final record in Canada (because all the Snakes' records were released on American independent labels, they were considered imports in Canada and often marked up in price). This was the closest the band came to the Canadian music establishment, and it immediately revealed itself as a poor fit.

"When we signed that licensing deal, they wanted us to do an interview with this in-flight magazine for an airline. They put us in touch with the person and she told us to come for a fitting. I said, 'What are you talking about? If you want to take our picture, fine, but we'll wear our own clothes.' She said, 'No, this is for a modeling gig. We need a band to wear clothes by a certain designer.' I said, 'I think you've got us mixed up with somebody else.'"

As the band wore on, and their chances of overnight success dwindled, they were even less inclined to want to run through the paces of promoting themselves in the industry. But even if they had been, by 2005 the Snakes didn't find touring worth the sacrifice it demanded of each member.

"We all had girlfriends, and we all had family," says Chad Ross. "I don't honestly feel that anyone ever wanted to give up their personal lives."

"Like André, getting married, buying a house: people wanted to grow up," says Moszynski.

CHAPTER 9
PORCELLA

"It felt like family." – Andrew Moszynski

NO ONE HAD SAID out loud that the band was ending when they gathered in Moszynski's parents' cabin to record *Porcella*, but as Ethier recalls, "I guess that's why we bothered trying to make it fun." They invested in first-rate food and liquor, beer and wine, and procured fresh vegetables from nearby Mennonite farmhouses. Even the wildlife ate well: the band bought two huge sacks of peanuts and vowed to feed them all to chipmunks before the week was over. In between takes they shot at targets with BB-guns and cut themselves pieces of prosciutto from the leg dangling above the mixing board.

Isolated in the country, they could play as late as they wanted. Over a 10-day recording period they practiced songs, reworked them and experimented with different approaches. Early in the day they'd work on mellow numbers, and after dinner and drinks, bang together the louder tracks.

After the day was done, they'd settle down to watch movies together as a group, each member having brought with him films that reflected his tastes. Moszynski, as the comedy of the band, brought DVDs of *Mr. Show*; the others brought a selection of titles, including *Quest for Fire*, after which Moszynski, Ross and engineer Josh Bauman would later name their follow up band. McCabe-Lokos, remembers Bauman, "brought the most pretentious art films you'd ever seen. This wasn't even first-year film school shit, like Fellini. He brought really weird stuff."

Importantly, they did everything as a group. They played, they ate, they played again, and finally they relaxed together, as The Deadly Snakes.

"It felt like family," Moszynski says.

Two weeks after the cabin recording session, Ethier married his longtime girlfriend Kai, but following the wedding, while the Ethiers were on their honeymoon, McCabe-Lokos began recording *Porcella*'s overdubs and vocals.

"Half the overdubs started when I was away," says Ethier. "In retrospect I think that was totally unnecessary. Max said in an interview that he saw that last record as his own solo record, but he never told us that he was thinking that way. I feel like he started the overdubs on purpose while I was away so he would have more control and direction."

Ethier explains that *Porcella* was the only Snakes album that had a vague central concept; while recording it, he says, "Max and I talked about consumption and depression— there's a lot of financial references in there. Debt, wealth, sadness." Strongly influenced by Leonard Cohen, Nick Cave and Nico's *Chelsea Girls*, the songs are mostly reflective and melancholy mid-tempo numbers characterized by strings and Van Morrison-style horn arrangement.

In the earlier days of the band, Ethier says, "someone would bring a song in and everyone would argue and fight about it until it became a Deadly Snakes song, and no longer that person's song. By *Porcella* it was more mercenary. Or at least, in our memory, it became that way."

"*Porcella* is the sound of a band breaking up," says Moszynski. "The way I hear the record is basically four guys—six guys, actually—wanting to take the band in different directions."

Yet it's also the record of McCabe-Lokos and Ethier at their best, each contributing a calibre of songwriting they'd only hinted at on previous records. McCabe-Lokos is finally the frontman of the band he's been leading for the preceding decade; he and Ethier each sings six songs, along with another track on which they share vocals with ex-Spaceshits frontman Mark "BBQ" Sultan.

Perhaps Ethier's album-opener "Debt Collection" says the most about his contributions to the record. "It was about owing allegiance to someone because of favours done," Ethier says. "I wrote it in reference to the band, and to some degree Max. I see it as unnecessarily petulant now, but I really felt the band was almost repressive by that point. I also see it as Max's doing that we had any drive to succeed. I learned how to achieve artistically from him and I felt guilty for being so pissed at him."

Ethier claims not to have adhered strongly to the album's theme, yet his songs return to the world seen through the jaded eyes of someone far older than anyone represented on a previous Snakes album, growing older and grimly facing adult responsibilities. Even his ostensible love song, "Oh Lord, My Heart!"—easily one of the album's best tracks—is a bleakly beautiful study in sorrow and futility that cautions, "If a man can't love when he is young, there'll be no love for him when he grows old."

McCabe-Lokos's songs deal less with the responsibilities of adulthood than with the emotions of dwindling youth and an uncertain future.

"If you took all them together on one CD," says Ethier of McCabe-Lokos's tracks on *Porcella*, "you'd see a portrayal of something really specific."

Principal among them is the stunning "Gore Veil,"[8] which McCabe-Lokos describes as being "about using violence as an escape from existential crisis. I was trying to write about this attitude where you accept total defeat." Borrowing style from "I Want to Die," the song is built around a cheery mellotron and backup vocals, against which McCabe-Lokos sings of being challenged by "the quivering frailty" of mortality and finding clarity "in the storm and the strife" of violence, finally concluding with the line, "What am I for, if not to die?"

This is a long way from "Pirate Cowboy," though McCabe-Lokos is quick to caution against reading his lyrics personally. He says, "I'm a pretty happy person, but it's just that the things I was interested in were more melancholy." This is a strong point, yet it remains tempting to read the song's expression of a sensitive character who finds meaning in conflict with others as personal.

The embrace of defeat is present in one way or another throughout the rest of McCabe-Lokos's songs on the album. Even "The Banquet," a possessed rave-up coupling images of surrender with celebration in which he ends on the line,

---

8 Its title a play on the name of Gore Vale Avenue in Toronto's west end.

"put your hand on my heart and feel it beat, because this is it: this is the last song, this is the last drink, and this is the last week of our lives."

Greg Cartwright calls *Porcella* his favourite of the Snakes' four records, citing the high quality of songwriting—especially McCabe-Lokos's. What's most startling, he says, is that the Snakes made their best record at the end of their career.

"How many bands make anything valid or anything you want to hear past their third record?" Cartwright asks. "Most bands say everything they have to say in two records, unless they're ready to grow, and that's what makes the Snakes special. All the obvious influences on the first record are almost gone by the last two records. They were ready to experiment with songwriting ideas, production ideas, instrumentation, and if you're ready to embrace that, you can make as many records as you want. Because that's growth."

The album's final track, "A Bird in the Hand is Worthless," is a disarmingly pretty song about loss and regret showcasing McCabe-Lokos's baritone atop a deftly chirping organ and streaming string section, grieving the passing of optimism and the pain of thinking back on better times from a point in the future after "the sunny days [are] gone/[…] all replaced by photographs and fibreglass and styrofoam."

It's a fitting and perfect end to the record, and seems to forecast the end of the band, though McCabe-Lokos is quick to caution, "Just because that's the image the record ended on, and it's a good image to end with, but the band also ended—they're not related. That's music on a record and this is guys playing music together. You can remark on the similarities, but they exist separately, on their own."

Taken as a whole, *Porcella*, though not as cohesive in songwriting as its members would have liked, is an exquisitely played and finely crafted record that would have been unimaginable five years earlier in the Snakes' career. It's worth noting that the two finest songs on the album, McCabe-Lokos's "Gore Veil" and Ethier's "Oh Lord, My Heart!" are the only two co-credited to Matt Carlson, whose brilliance lends much to the complexity and subtlety of their arrangement. Likewise, the uncredited contribution of the Snakes as a group to the songwriting is abundant—especially in moments like Ross's outstanding mandolin line on "By Morning It's Gone" or Carlson's arrangement of horns in the same song. During the recording of the first album only six years before, Moszynski had to tape foam over his cymbals because he hit them too hard; by contrast, *Porcella* seems not only lyrically but also musically the product of years of growing up.

———

After *Porcella* was released—to considerable acclaim from the independent press, including another high rating from Pitchfork—the band set out to tour again, in support of an album without a single that wasn't selling very well. In contrast to other major forces in Canadian indie music, the Snakes' wild energy, coarse roots and dedication to expanding rock and roll tradition never appealed to commercial audiences.

"We weren't playing music like the Arcade Fire that makes people feel pumped when they're exercising or walking to work," Ethier says. "We weren't particularly catchy or anthemic. It was stuff that doesn't connect."

Ethier doesn't blame anyone for the Snakes' lack of commercial success, pointing out that the band received media attention in Canada and had great chances such as the tours with Sloan and the Hives.

"We had every opportunity to be popular," he says. "It's just that our music doesn't connect with a lot of people. It connects with a certain type of music fan, looking for a certain type of sound. You could have put our videos on MuchMusic in heavy rotation, and I still don't think it would connect. I think—and I mean this in the most positive way—we have too much personality, and because of our large personality, the conflict, which I think shows through in the music, is too colourful. There's positive and engaging stuff, but there's also darkness. And there's well played parts, and badly played parts, all mixed together. It's too messy."

Early mentor Chris Trowbridge, however, bristles at what he feels was a lack of interest from the Canadian music establishment, recalling that all of the Snakes' albums were released through two small labels in Los Angeles.

"They didn't send out demos or anything," he says, "But no Canadian label ever showed a sliver of fucking interest in them. They were an independent band."

Between the Deadly Snakes' lack of interest in touring and the lack of interest from audiences, the *Porcella* tour made clear what they had suspected during recording: they were at the end.

The band's lowest point occurred in October of 2005, when they played a sports bar in Thunder Bay, Ontario. Between poor promotion and confusion between local promoters, the show went unadvertised and nobody came out.

"There are some shows when only 10 people show up," Ethier says, "and you think *maybe we shouldn't play it*, but you do, and you feel great because you did it and those people liked it. You're happy you played. But that one—the bar left the TVs on, and all of us were watching TV while we played."

Because they were watching TV, they all noticed when the film *The Big Bounce* came on, featuring their song "Everybody Seems to Think (You've Got Some Kind of Hold on Me)," subjecting them to a kind of cosmic joke of cable programming.

"There were so many TVs in this cavernous, empty sports bar," says Chad Ross. "All playing it."

Ethier shakes his head. "Thunder Bay is so fucking far away, too. To drive all the way there for that."

A few months later, the band decided it was time to quit: they were broke, losing money by taking time off work to tour, and weren't getting any bigger. They did a final, celebratory tour of Europe as a farewell to one another.

"We celebrated breaking up by going to Europe," says Ross. "Everyone knew it was our last tour and mellowed out, so we had a great time. It was three weeks, but I'd have gladly done six."

Following their return from Europe, they organized their final show, which occurred in late August of 2006, 10 years after the band was supposed to have ended after the laundromat gig. They billed it widely as the last time they would play together.

"It was kind of ballsy to announce it," says Chris Trowbridge. "I said to them, 'You don't have to say it's your last show, you can always keep your options open,' but they said, 'It'd be a really good party.'" I thought it was a cool gesture, but then it's shooting yourself in the foot, because you can't be the Deadly Snakes anymore. But it's honest! They didn't want to do it anymore, so they were going to say that, and it was the right thing for them to do."

There were, in fact, two final Deadly Snakes shows: the official last show at Toronto's Horseshoe Tavern, featuring two long sets recorded for posterity, and the unannounced actual last show the next night, booked by Dan Burke a few blocks up the street at the Silver Dollar Room. The first night was more careful. McCabe-Lokos recalls, "I was thinking, *Oh my god, are we playing okay? Am I having fun? I've gotta have fun!* I went backstage and drank a bunch of whiskey and barfed or something. Then after that, I decided, *I'm gonna have fun now!* But there wasn't enough abandon." The next night, consisting of a set largely composed of requests shouted from an audience of friends, was a lot looser.

"It was super fun and friendly," McCabe-Lokos says. "There was a lot of love. By the time we did the last song, it was a drunken mess—we were high and drunk like it didn't matter."

As they prepared for their farewell show, the band had learned that *Porcella* had been nominated for the first-ever Polaris Music Prize, a juried award given to a Canadian full-length album judged the best of the year "based on artistic merit, regardless of genre, sales or record label." It was the first moment in the band's career that they had received any official attention from the Canadian music industry, and it came too late. No one in the band had any illusions that they would beat critical darlings Broken Social Scene, Wolf

Parade, the New Pornographers or Final Fantasy (who won). The awards ceremony was just weeks after the final Snakes shows. Dragged onstage to represent the band as nominees, Ethier told the room with a chuckle, "I guess it's no secret that we broke up last month. *Maybe that's a burn on us; maybe that's a burn on you.*"

Ethier remembers, "Polaris was in September, and our last show was at the end of August, first week of September, so the guy from [distributor] Paper Bag, the fucking idiot, said, 'Don't announce that your last show is your last show so you can play at the Polaris. It'll increase your chances of winning.' He was asking us to completely undermine any integrity behind the last show we were having just so we could play three songs and try to win this stupid Canadian prize. It was such shucking and jiving. So we just went and didn't win. Of course we didn't."

CHAPTER 10

OH LORD, MY HEART

"The Snakes were a compressed typical history of rock and roll." – Chris Trowbridge

IN THE WAKE of the band's dissolution, the ex-Snakes were left in various emotional states. Moszynski recalls being miserable for months after the breakup.

"It's hard to break up the band you grew up in," he says. "The one thing I was good at was playing Deadly Snakes songs and I couldn't do that anymore. It was pretty obvious that we couldn't make another record, but it was really hard to make the decision of *this has to stop*."

"At first," says McCabe-Lokos, "I was *so* happy, like I was ending a bad relationship and I was single again. It was really nice to be an individual, not part of a group. For the first year or so, I was relishing that, and it felt really free and good. But then I started looking back and thinking, *Jeez, that was kind of fun*. Now I look back and remember a lot of good moments. There are times when I kind of miss playing live—some shows were really invigorating. But never once would I ever feel like getting on stage and playing with that band again."

McCabe-Lokos, like everyone else, agrees that "everybody's happy that it ended when it did, because it could have been that we couldn't have been friends. There are no grudges that lasted. There was some ugliness, but the reason we broke up was that it started to become just a little less friendly. I was probably becoming sort of intolerable, and it wasn't worth tolerating, where there'd been a point where earlier it was."

"We went on a fantastic adventure," says Ethier with a self-effacing laugh. "But then it had to end. All the things that might have been great about it would have become depressing. Like any band, you have to ride this wave and you have to know where the high-water mark is, and you usually go past it and you're receding. The trick is to get off the wave before you go too far down. Especially if you're not successful. If we'd been successful and making a lot of money, we would have had a responsibility to our spouses and to ourselves to figure out a way of maintaining that."

"The Snakes were a compressed typical history of rock and roll," says Chris Trowbridge. "They were this really basic band, really in debt to black music, then they got more poppy, and more pretentious, and bloated, then they couldn't keep going. They went from 1964 to 1970, like the Kinks or anybody, from being this great little powerhouse to this song about fucking nautical miles, and strings, the whole fucking bit. It was a cliché to have that progression. But I think it's cool, it's what everybody's done—it's this little microcosm of popular music."

The Snakes are unanimous in agreeing that they got exactly what they deserved.

"We never put all that much effort into it," says Moszynski. "We could have pushed it, stayed on the road 10 months a year. For the amount of work we put in, we got an incredible return."

Ethier clarifies, "We put a lot of hard work into the band, but all of it went into music and performing and things that are actually rewarding."

"Considering the amount of shit that didn't get done properly," McCabe-Lokos says wryly, "the amount of fighting, and the amount of unwillingness to succeed that we had, I think that it evens out."

Chad Ross responds to the occasional question from a fan who wanted the band to last longer by expressing his gratitude for its successful end. "I think it might be a blessing in disguise that we broke up when we did," he says. "I'm still a huge Snakes fan—I love those records dearly. There aren't a lot of people who can say that after their band breaks up."

Moszynski adds, "We could tour until the end of time if we wanted to and I'm sure people would still show up, but the band didn't work the way it used to. It didn't seem to be something we could carry on and also be grown-ups—it started to seem maybe that it was best left as *the way* we grew up. We could walk away from it knowing that we're now different people with a lot of stories to tell."

Reflecting on the Snakes' relative lack of success, Greg Cartwright explains, "What you're due is for history to look back and see what was the best. If you're not a legend in your own time, don't be surprised. People always discover what is truly great after the fact. That's just the way it is. And that's your due. That's the beautiful payoff of music. Hopefully these records will remain to be things that people cite as some of the best music from that decade. If you get that, for any artist, that is payment enough."

Max McCabe-Lokos is right: the end of a band is not like the end of a record, which can be designed to express some final statement. Bands just end when they can no longer maintain whatever it is that drove them to play together in the first place, and usually they end without much of a gesture. Yet the ends of friendships are even stranger, even less defined. To this day, the Deadly Snakes remain friends, though they see one another less frequently than they did as a band.

All have wives or serious girlfriends; some own their houses. They have long since ceased to be a musical gang and have become other, calmer things; their albums are the only record of what they once were.

EPILOGUE

"IT'S LAME TO do things for money," says Max McCabe-Lokos. "I don't have a huge moral opposition to doing things for money, but it doesn't feel comfortable. I don't like it when bands reform. I think it's fucking bullshit across the board, it's a chickenshit thing to do. If you're going to be a band, you should make records. All these bands that have a big breakup and then when the demand is hot enough they reform and just tour ad nauseam, like the Pixies or Pavement, I think it's cowardly, and I felt like an impostor when I was doing it."

In the fall of 2009, as I was in the early stages of putting this book together, I received the startling news that the Deadly Snakes were booked to play a reunion show at the Scion Garage Rock Fest in Portland, Oregon. Organized by *Vice* magazine, the free festival was set up as a branding exercise for Toyota's Scion line of vehicles, whose target market is young people.[9] According to *Bloomberg*, the brand was in-

---

9 Scion has since put significant effort into associating itself with independent music, going so far as to set up the Scion Audio/Visual art and music marketing wing, promoting shows and releasing recordings by artists ranging from metal to hip hop to electronic. In the fall of 2011, Scion A/V released a free-to-download EP by Greg Cartwright's the Reigning Sound, *Abdication ... For Your Love*. However you may feel about the unholy mix of marketing and music, that EP is killer.

tended "to lure young U.S. buyers [...] with new cars aimed more at boosting the brand's hipness than sales."

The festival line-up was spectacular, from eminent headliner Roky Erikson, to long-lost R&B star Gino Washington, on down. Convincing the Snakes to reform for the festival was a coup (which the festival would repeat the next year by convincing the legendary Oblivians to reform), but the roster was strong from top to bottom, featuring favourites like the Dirtbombs, the Pierced Arrows, the Black Lips and Jay Reatard (who died three months later), but also boasting talented newer acts like the Mannequin Men, Goodnight Loving, Davila 666, the Intelligence and Thomas Function.[10]

Naturally I wanted to go, but as I had been when the Snakes played their last shows in Toronto three years before, I was broke. It remained for me to catch up with Andrew Moszynski and Chad Ross the next time they toured through Montreal with Quest for Fire. When I arrived at their show, I immediately found Andrew and asked him about Portland. He laughed sardonically and told me that while everyone had had a good time, the show itself had sealed the deal— the Snakes were finished.

In August, 2012, when I asked him again about the experience, he said, "We all had a good time doing it, but it did maybe shine a light on why we stopped playing as a band. I had a great time, and we were treated really, really well. There were just enough little things to serve as reminders that there was a reason we all agreed to stop."

Max McCabe-Lokos is, not surprisingly, the bluntest in his

---

10 These last five are just my favourites of the newer bands that played the festival. There were 43 groups on the bill, many very good and very popular.

description of the experience. He says they initially refused to reform, but then decided to suggest what seemed like an absurd amount of money, to which the festival agreed.

"We said, 'Oh shit, I guess we have to do it now.' So then we did it, and it was lame."

"It might sound callous," McCabe-Lokos continues, "but we just said we'll do it for $10,000. It was only for money. I'm not happy about it. I didn't like it. I like seeing those guys and taking a trip to Portland—it was a fun weekend. But I did not like it and it will never happen again. As soon as I got on stage I was like, 'Oh fuck, this is gonna be a race to get off.'"

"We had no agenda other than to have a good time," says André Ethier. "We weren't reigniting our career. We met as friends and individuals and played a show, rather than the Snakes playing a show. I remember being really excited. We were proud to be offered that money. It was nice to get paid after all those years. And also to go somewhere—it was a vacation together. We saw people we hadn't seen in a long time, and met bands we hadn't met before but were fans of."

Comparing the occasion to a group of "fat and bald" old friends getting together to go fishing, McCabe-Lokos pauses and says, "Actually, that would have been more fun. But it's cool, because everybody in that band, we're all friends and it's not that often that we all get to hang out together. Some of the more caustic behaviour between members of the band is long since extinguished. I'm really close with André and Matt. Our friendship is so much more important than ever playing a show again. So as a group of guys, it was fun to hang out together in Portland and see some friends we hadn't seen in a few years."

The difference between touring and just taking a vacation with friends, says Moszynski, is that "If you've [toured] a bunch of times, every night you're seeing your friends from out of town. They're all going to congregate at your show. That's different from just going on vacation—there's no event, nothing to bring everyone together. I'm so glad we did it, just for one last taste of it. I think it was definitely the right thing to do. The people who put it together were people who'd never seen us before, and for them, we were one of their top-of-the-list favourite bands. They genuinely cared. I'd never shut the door on doing stuff like that again, but that's obviously up to everybody, not just me."

"It didn't feel, at the end, like we should get back together," says Ethier. "If anything, it really ended the band."

"It doesn't really matter," concludes McCabe-Lokos. "We're generally agreed that it wasn't the best show and wasn't really worth it. I just kind of erase it. You know, 'Oh yeah, that? Whatever.' It's kind of like you and your girlfriend break up—let's say you move to different cities and haven't seen your girlfriend from ten years ago, and when you run into her, you think, 'Wow! She looks really good! And she's recently divorced!' And then you get drunk one night and have sex, and the next day you're like, 'Well, *that's* never going to fucking happen again.'"